저자 **이 종 저**

이화여자대학교 졸업
Longman Grammar Joy 1, 2, 3, 4권
Longman Vocabulary Mentor Joy 1, 2, 3권
I am Grammar 1, 2권
Grammar & Writing Level A 1, 2권 / Level B 1, 2권
Polybooks Grammar joy start 1, 2, 3, 4권
Polybooks Grammar joy 1, 2, 3, 4권
Polybooks 기본을 잡아주는 중등 영문법 1a,1b,2a,2b,3a,3b권
Polybooks 문법을 잡아주는 영작 1, 2, 3, 4권
Polybooks Grammar joy & Writing 1, 2, 3, 4권
Polybooks Bridging 초등 Voca 1, 2권
Polybooks Joy 초등 Voca 1, 2권

감수 **Jeanette Lee**

Wellesley college 졸업

지은이 | 이종저
펴낸곳 | POLY books
펴낸이 | POLY 영어 교재 연구소
기 획 | 박정원
편집디자인 | 이은경
삽화 | 이수진
초판 1쇄 인쇄 | 2015년 4월 25일
초판 22쇄 발행 | 2023년 2월 10일

POLY 영어 교재 연구소
경기도 성남시 분당구 황새울로 200번길 28 1128호
전화 070-7799-1583
ISBN | 979-11-86924-25-9
         979-11-86924-23-5(set)

Grammar joy 1

Preface

그 동안 Grammar Mentor Joy에 보내 주신 아낌없는 사랑과 관심에 힘입어 저자가 직접 Grammar Joy 시리즈의 개정판을 출간하게 되었습니다. 이에 더욱 학생들의 효과적인 학습에 도움이 될 수 있도록 연구개발하여 새롭게 선보이게 되었습니다.

영어 문법을 쉽고 재미있게 가르치고 배우길 바라며

본 개정판은 이전 학습자 및 선생님들의 의견과 영어 시장의 새로운 흐름에 맞춰 현장 교육을 바탕으로 집필하였습니다.

Grammar Joy는 다년간 현장 교육을 바탕으로, 학생의 눈높이와 학습 패턴에 맞춘 개념 설명, 재미있고 능동적이며 반복학습을 통해 자신도 모르는 사이에 영어 어휘와 문법을 익혀 나갈 수 있도록 합니다.

기본기를 확실히 다지도록 합니다

학생들은 대체로, 처음엔 영어에 흥미를 가지다가도 일정 시간이 흐르면 점차 어려워하고 지겹게 느끼기 시작합니다. 하지만, 기본 실력을 다지고 어느 정도 영어에 흥미를 계속 유지하도록 지도하면 어느 순간 실력이 월등해지고 재미를 붙여 적극성을 띄게 되는 것이 영어 학습입니다. Grammar Joy는 영어 학습에 꾸준히 흥미를 가질 수 있도록 기본기를 다져 줍니다.

어려운 정통 문법은 나중으로 미룹니다

영어에도 공식이 있습니다. 물론 실력자들은 공식이 아니라 어법이라고 하지요. 하지만 처음부터 어려운 어법을 강요하기보다는 쉬운 수학문제처럼, 어휘의 활용과 어순을 쉽게 이해할 수 있도록 규칙적인 해법을 공식화할 필요가 있습니다. 매우 단순해 보이지만 이를 반복 학습하다보면 어느새 공식의 개념을 깨닫게 되고 나중엔 그 공식에 얽매이지 않고 스스로 활용할 수 있게 됩니다. 이 책에서 쉬운 문제를 집중해서 푸는 것이 바로 그 공식을 소화해 가는 과정이라고 할 수 있습니다.

생동감있는 다양한 문장들로 이루어져 있습니다

실생활에서도 자주 쓰이는 문장들로 구성하여 현장 학습효과를 낼 수 있도록 하였습니다.

최고보다는 꼭 필요한 교재이고자 합니다

다년간 현장 교육을 통해, 학생들이 기존 문법 체계에 적응하기 어려워한다는 사실을 발견하였습니다. 학생들의 눈높이에 맞춰 흥미로운 학습 내용을 다루면서 자연스럽게 문법과 연계되는 내용들을 다루었습니다. 특히 이번 개정판은 기본을 잡아주는 중등 영문법(Grammar Joy Plus)와 연계하여 중학교 내신에 대비에 부족함이 없도록 내용을 구성하였으므로 Grammar Joy를 끝내고 기본을 잡아주는 중등 영문법(Grammar Joy Plus)를 공부한다면, 쓸데없는 중복 학습을 피하고 알찬 중학과정의 grammar 까지 완성할 수 있을 것이라 믿습니다.

모쪼록, 이 교재를 통해 선생님과 학생들이 재미있고 흥미있는 학습으로 소기의 성과를 얻을 수 있기를 기대하며 그동안 이번 시리즈를 출간하느라 함께 이해하며 동행해 주었던 이은경님께 아울러 감사드립니다.

저자 이종저

Contents

Series Contents

Guide to This Book

1 Unit별 핵심정리

가장 기초적인 문법 사항과 핵심 포인트를 알기 쉽게 제시하여 주의 환기 및 개념 이해를 돕습니다.

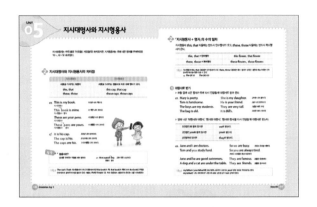

2 기초 다지기

Unit별 핵심 내용에 대한 매우 기초적인 확인 문제로, 개념 이해 및 스스로 문제를 풀어 보는 연습을 할 수 있도록 합니다.

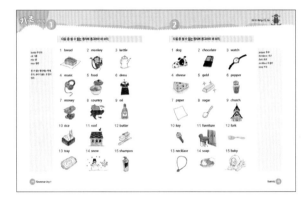

3 꼭꼭 다지기

기초 다지기보다 다소 난이도 있는 연습문제로, 앞서 배운 내용을 복습할 수 있도록 합니다.

4 실력 다지기

다양한 형태로 제시되는 확장형 응용문제를 통해 문법 개념을 확실히 이해하고 실력을 굳힐 수 있도록 합니다.

5 실전 테스트

Unit별 마무리 테스트로서, 해당 Unit에서 배운 모든 문법 개념이 적용된 문제 풀이를 통해 응용력을 키우고 학교 선행학습에 대비할 수 있도록 합니다.

6 Quiz

한 Unit이 끝난 뒤에 쉬어가는 페이지로서, 앞서 배운 내용을 퀴즈 형태로 재미있게 풀어보고 다음 Unit로 넘어갈 수 있도록 합니다.

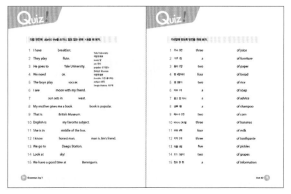

7 Review 테스트, 내신 대비

그 동안 배운 내용을 다시 한 번 복습할 수 있도록 이미 학습한 Unit에 대한 주관식 문제와 내신 대비를 위한 객관식 문제들을 풀어 보도록 합니다.

8 종합문제

최종 마무리 테스트로서, Unit 1~8 전체에 대한 종합적인 학습 내용을 다시 한번 점검하고 취약 부분을 파악할 수 있도록 합니다.

How to Use This Book

Grammar Joy Series는 전체 4권으로 구성되었으며, 각 권당 6주, 총 6개월의 수업 분량으로 기획되었습니다. 학습자와 학습 시간의 차이에 따라 문제 풀이 단계가운데 일부를 과제로 부여하거나 보충 수업을 통하여 시수를 맞출 수 있도록 하였습니다. 또한, 아래 제시된 진행 방식 외에, 학생들이 취약한 학습 영역을 다룬 교재를 먼저 채택하여 수업하실 수도 있습니다.

Month	Course	Week	Hour	Curriculum (Unit)	Homework/ Extra Curriculum
1st Month	Joy 1	1st	1	1. 셀 수 있는 명사	▶각 Unit별 퀴즈
			2		▶시수별 단어 풀이 과제 부여 또는 수업 중 단어 실력 테스트
			3		
	Joy 1	2nd	1	2. 셀 수 없는 명사	▶Review Test 내신대비
			2		
			3	3. 관사	
	Joy 1	3rd	1		
			2	4. 인칭대명사와 지시대명사	
			3		
	Joy 1	4th	1	5. 지시대명사와 지시형용사	
			2		
			3		
2nd Month	Joy 1	1st	1	6. 인칭대명사의 격변화	
			2		
			3		
	Joy 1	2nd	1	7. be동사의 긍정문	
			2	8. be동사의 부정문, 의문문	
			3		
	Joy 2	3rd	1	1. There is~/There are~	▶각 Unit별 퀴즈
			2		▶시수별 단어 풀이 과제 부여 또는 수업 중 단어 실력 테스트
			3	2. 일반동사의 긍정문	
	Joy 2	4th	1		▶Review Test 내신대비
			2	3. 일반동사의 부정문과 의문문	
			3		
3rd Month	Joy 2	1st	1	4. 현재진행형	
			2		
			3		
	Joy 2	2nd	1	5. 형용사	
			2		
			3		
	Joy 2	3rd	1	6. some, any와 many, much, a lot of	
			2		
			3	7. 부사	
	Joy 2	4th	1		
			2	8. 비교	
			3		

Month	Course	Week	Hour	Curriculum (Unit)	Homework/ Extra Curriculum
4th Month	Joy 3	1st	1 2 3	**1.** 「의문사 + 일반동사」 의문문	▶ 각 Unit별 퀴즈 ▶ 시수별 단어 풀이 과제 부여 또는 수업 중 단어 실력 테스트 ▶ Review Test 내신대비
	Joy 3	2nd	1 2 3	**2.** 「의문사 + be동사」 의문문 **3.** 의문대명사와 의문형용사	
	Joy 3	3rd	1 2 3	**4.** 의문부사(1)	
	Joy 3	4th	1 2 3	**5.** 의문부사(2) **6.** 접속사와 명령문	
5th Month	Joy 3	1st	1 2 3	**7.** 조동사(can, must)	
	Joy 3	2nd	1 2 3	**8.** 전치사	
	Joy 4	3rd	1 2 3	**1.** 기수, 서수 **2.** 비인칭주어	▶ 각 Unit별 퀴즈 ▶ 시수별 단어 풀이 과제 부여 또는 수업 중 단어 실력 테스트 ▶ Review Test 내신대비 ▶ 종합문제
	Joy 4	4th	1 2 3	**3.** be동사, 일반동사 과거형의 긍정문	
6th Month	Joy 4	1st	1 2 3	**4.** 과거형의 부정문, 의문문	
	Joy 4	2nd	1 2 3	**5.** 과거진행형	
	Joy 4	3rd	1 2 3	**6.** 미래형 **7.** 감탄문	
	Joy 4	4th	1 2 3	**8.** 부정의문문, 부가의문문	

Practice makes perfect.

Unit 01

셀 수 있는 명사

사람이나 사물의 이름을 나타내는 말을
명사라 한다. 명사는 셀 수 있는 명사와
셀 수 없는 명사로 나눌 수 있는데,
셀 수 있는 명사는 수가 하나이면
단수형으로, 둘 이상이면
복수형으로 나타낸다.

셀 수 있는 명사

명사란?

의미   사람이나 사물의 이름을 나타내는 말이다.
       ex. desk, chair, pen, bag …

종류   ❶ 셀 수 있는 명사   *ex.* book, pen, ball, family, team, class …
       ❷ 셀 수 없는 명사   *ex.* water, money, juice, rain …

➊ 단수와 복수

① 단수

명사의 개수가 하나인 것을 말한다.

ex. book, desk, girl …

② 복수

명사의 개수가 둘 이상인 것을 말한다.
우리말에서는 복수를 말할 때 「~들」로 나타내지만
영어에서는 단어 끝에 s나 es를 붙여, 복수형을 나타낸다.

ex. books, desks, girls …

한글에도 자음 (ㄱ, ㄴ, ㄷ, ㄹ, ㅁ,…) 과 모음 (ㅏ, ㅑ, ㅓ, ㅕ, ㅗ,…) 이 있듯이 영어에도 자음 (b, c, d, f, g, h, …) 과 모음 (a, e, i, o, u) 이 있다.

복수형 만드는 방법

① 규칙 변화

열 번씩 큰소리로 읽어 보자. ○○○○○ ○○○○○

공식		예	
대부분의 명사	+ s	pen → pens	nurse → nurses
자음 + y로 끝날 때	y → ies	city → cities	lady → ladies
f(e)로 끝날 때	f(e) → ves	knife → knives	leaf → leaves
	예외(+s)	chef → chefs scarf → scarfs	chief → chiefs roof → roofs
o, s, x, sh, ch로 끝날 때	+ es	potato → potatoes dress → dresses watch → watches	bus → buses box → boxes dish → dishes
	예외(+s)	memo → memos video → videos cello → cellos	photo → photos piano → pianos zoo → zoos

city 도시
lady 숙녀
knife 칼
leaf 잎
chef 요리사
chief 최고위자
roof 지붕

> hero
> → heroes
> mosquito
> → mosquitos
>   mosquitoes
> soprano
> → sopranos
> alto
> → altos

* scarf의 복수형의 경우 scarves로도 쓰인다.

② 불규칙 변화

열 번씩 큰소리로 읽어 보자. ○○○○○ ○○○○○

모음만 바뀌는 경우	oo → ee	foot → feet goose → geese	tooth → teeth
	a → e	man → men	woman → women
모양이 일부 바뀌는 경우	+ en + ren	ox → oxen child → children	
	ouse → ice	mouse → mice	
단수, 복수 모양이 같은 경우	fish → fish deer → deer sheep → sheep Japanese → Japanese Chinese → Chinese		
복수형만 있는 경우	people		

foot 발
tooth 이, 치아
goose 거위
man 남자
woman 여자
ox 황소
child 아이
mouse 쥐
fish (물)고기
deer 사슴
sheep 양
Japanese 일본사람
Chinese 중국사람
people 사람

> **Tip!** fish는 같은 종류의 물고기를 복수로 나타낼 때는 fish로 단수와 복수의 형태가 같지만, 각기 다른 물고기들의
> 종류를 복수로 나타낼 때는 fishes가 된다.

마지막 철자 부분에 유의하여 다음 빈칸에 명사의 복수형을 규칙에 따라 써 보자.

lady 숙녀
chef 요리사 (특히 주방장)
memo 메모

1 cup + s = *cups*

2 hat + s =

3 house + s =

4 nurse + s =

5 city + ies = *cities*

6 lady + ies =

7 baby + ies =

8 country + ies =

9 boy + s =

10 toy + s =

11 knife + ves = *knives*

12 leaf + ves =

13 wife + ves =

14 wolf + ves =

15 chef + s = *chefs*

16 chief + s =

17 scarf + s =

18 roof + s =

19 potato + es = *potatoes*

20 tomato + es =

21 bus + es =

22 box + es =

23 dress + es =

24 dish + es =

25 memo + s = *memos*

26 photo + s =

27 video + s =

28 piano + s =

29 cello + s =

30 zoo + s =

2

규칙변화를 하는 명사의 복수형을 만드는 방법과 이에 해당하는 단어들을
|보기|에서 골라 연결해 보자.

| 보기 |　A.　knife, leaf, wolf, wife

　　　　　B.　chef, chief, scarf, roof

　　　　　C.　city, lady, country, candy

　　　　　D.　potato, tomato, bus, dress, glass, box, watch, dish

　　　　　E.　pen, nurse, house, ball, table

　　　　　F.　memo, photo, video, piano, cello, zoo

knife 칼
leaf 나뭇잎
chief 의장
scarf 스카프
roof 지붕
memo 메모
photo 사진

1　+ s　　　　　　　　　　　　　　*E*

2　y → ies

3　f(e) → ves

4　f(e)로 끝나지만 + s

5　+ es

6　o로 끝나지만 + s

다음은 규칙변화를 하는 명사의 복수형이다. (   ) 안에서 알맞은 것에 동그라미 해 보자.

watch 시계
city 도시
brother 남자형제
dish 접시
potato 감자
glass 유리잔

* 문제 풀기 전에 다음을
  꼭 확인하자.
  단어의 끝이 무엇으로
  끝나는지 확인한다.
  불규칙 변화 명사인지
  확인한다.
  단어의 끝이 「자음+y」
  이면 y를 ies로 바꿔준다.
  단어의 끝이 f(e)이면
  f(e)를 ves로 바꿔 준다.
  단어가 o, x, s, ch, sh로
  끝나면 es를 붙인다.
  위의 경우에 해당하지
  않으면 s만 붙여 준다.

1   map   (maps, mapes)

2   bus   (buses, buss)

3   box   (boxs, boxes)

4   boy   (boys, boies)

5   watch   (watchs, watches)

6   knife   (knives, knifes)

7   city   (citys, cities)

8   cello   (celloes, cellos)

9   brother   (brotheres, brothers)

10   memo   (memos, memoes)

11   leaf   (leafs, leaves)

12   scarf   (scarves, scarfs)

13   dish   (dishes, dishs)

14   potato   (potatos, potatoes)

15   glass   (glasses, glasss)

4

다음은 규칙변화를 하는 명사의 복수형이다. (   ) 안에서 알맞은 것에 동그라미 해 보자.

1 video   (videoes, (videos))

2 candy   (candys, candies)

3 wolf   (wolves, wolfes)

4 nurse   (nurses, nursees)

5 piano   (pianos, pianoes)

6 photo   (photos, photoes)

7 desk   (desks, deskes)

8 church   (churches, churchs)

9 wife   (wifes, wives)

10 monkey   (monkeys, monkies)

11 chef   (cheves, chefs)

12 lion   (lions, liones)

13 country   (countries, countys)

14 roof   (rooves, roofs)

15 zoo   (zoos, zooes)

candy 사탕
church 교회
wife 부인
church 교회
monkey 원숭이
country 나라
roof 지붕
zoo 동물원

eraser 지우개
cellphone 휴대전화
butterfly 나비
tray 쟁반
glass 유리잔

1 leaf （(leaves), leafs）

2 chief （chieves, chiefs）

3 dress （dress, dresses）

4 eraser （erasers, eraseres）

5 potato （potatos, potatoes）

6 cell phone （cell phons, cell phones）

7 lady （ladies, ladys）

8 knife （knifes, knives）

9 chef （cheves, chefs）

10 picture （pictures, picturs）

11 butterfly （butterflys, butterflies）

12 tray （trays, traies）

13 bed （bedes, beds）

14 dish （dishs, dishes）

15 glass （glass, glasses）

6

다음은 규칙변화를 하는 명사의 복수형이다. ( ) 안에서 알맞은 것에 동그라미 해 보자.

1 brush   (brushes, brushs)

2 toy   (toies, toys)

3 lily   (lilys, lilies)

4 tomato   (tomatos, tomatoes)

5 dish   (dishes, dish)

6 student   (studentes, students)

7 scarf   (scarves, scarfs)

8 chair   (chaires, chairs)

9 zoo   (zoos, zooes)

10 kid   (kides, kids)

11 church   (churches, churchs)

12 fox   (foxes, foxs)

13 class   (class, classes)

14 wife   (wives, wifes)

15 country   (countries, countrys)

brush 솔
toy 장난감
lily 백합
dish 접시
kid 아이
class 반, 수업

규칙변화를 하는 명사의 복수형을 써 보자.

vase 꽃병
video 비디오
fox 여우
window 창문

1 a vase   two   *vases*

2 one dog   three

3 a city   two

4 a video   five

5 a knife   ten

6 one bus   six

7 a memo   four

8 one spoon   two

9 a fox   seven

10 one potato   four

11 a window   two

12 a country   nine

13 one zoo   three

14 a roof   six

15 one dish   three

8

규칙변화를 하는 명사의 복수형을 써 보자.

1	a roommate	five	*roommates*
2	a watch	three	
3	a knife	two	
4	one box	ten	
5	a nurse	six	
6	a piano	two	
7	one photo	nine	
8	a chief	two	
9	a baby	four	
10	a thief	eight	
11	a lady	seven	
12	one ruler	three	
13	one chef	six	
14	a dress	five	
15	a cello	ten	

roommate 룸메이트,
같은 방을 사용하는 사람
nurse 간호사
thief 도둑
ruler 자

다음은 불규칙변화를 하는 명사의 복수형이다. 변화하는 부분에 유의하여 복수형을 완성해 보자.

foot 발
man 남자
woman 여자
salesman 판매원
child 어린이
mouse 쥐
ox 황소
sheep 양
deer 사슴
fish 물고기

1 foot + ee =   *feet*   **2** tooth + ee =

3 goose + ee =   **4** man + e =   *men*

5 woman + e =   **6** sportsman + e =

7 salesman + e =   **8** policeman + e =

9 fisherman + e =   **10** gentleman + e =

11 mailman + e =   **12** ox + en =   *oxen*

13 child + ren =   **14** mouse + ice =

15 fish + =   *fish*   **16** deer + =

17 sheep + =   **18** Japanese + =

19 Chinese + =   **20** people + =

2

불규칙변화를 하는 명사의 복수형을 만드는 방법과 이에 해당하는
단어들을 |보기|에서 골라 연결해 보자.

| 보기 | A. people
   　　B. child, ox
   　　C. foot, tooth, goose
   　　D. mouse
   　　E. fish, deer, sheep, Japanese, Chinese
   　　F. man, woman, postman, policeman,
   　　　　fisherman, sportsman

---

people 사람들
child 어린이
ox 황소
Japanese 일본사람
Chinese 중국사람
fisherman 어부

1 모음만 바뀌는 경우 : oo → ee　　　　　　　　　C

2 모음만 바뀌는 경우 : a → e

3 모양이 일부 바뀌는 경우 : +ren, en

4 모양이 일부 바뀌는 경우 : ouse → ice

5 단수, 복수 모양이 같은 경우

6 복수형만 있는 경우

다음은 불규칙변화를 하는 명사의 복수형이다. ( ) 안에서 알맞은 것에 동그라미 해 보자.

man 사람
gentleman 신사
Englishman 영국사람
foot 발
tooth 이

1 fish   (fishs, fish)

2 child   (children, childs)

3 man   (men, man)

4 sheep   (sheeps, sheep)

5 people   (people, peoples)

6 ox   (oxen, oxes)

7 gentleman   (gentlemen, gentleman)

8 Chinese   (Chineses, Chinese)

9 Englishman   (Englishmen, Englishmans)

10 deer   (deer, deers)

11 foot   (foots, feet)

12 tooth   (teeth, tooths)

13 mouse   (mouses, mice)

14 Japanese   (Japanese, Japaneses)

15 goose   (gooses, geese)

4

다음은 불규칙변화를 하는 명사의 복수형이다. (   ) 안에서 알맞은 것에
동그라미 해 보자.

1 woman   (womans, women)

2 sheep   (sheeps, sheep)

3 policeman   (policemen, policeman)

4 deer   (deer, deers)

5 tooth   (tooths, teeth)

6 Chinese   (Chinese, Chineses)

7 child   (children, childs)

8 fish   (fishs, fish)

9 people   (people, peoples)

10 postman   (postmen, postmans)

11 foot   (foots, feet)

12 goose   (geese, gooses)

13 mouse   (mouses, mice)

14 ox   (oxen, oxs)

15 fish   (fishes, fish)

sheep 양
policeman 남자경찰관
policewoman 여자경찰관
goose 거위

다음 불규칙 변화를 하는 명사의 복수형을 써 보자.

mouse 쥐
mailman 집배원
sportsman 운동선수

1   a sheep   six   *sheep*

2   a man   three

3   one mouse   five

4   a Japanese   four

5   people   two

6   one ox   nine

7   a goose   four

8   a fish   seven

9   a mailman   ten

10 one Chinese   eight

11 a foot   two

12 one tooth   six

13 a child   five

14 a sportsman   two

15 one deer   three

6

다음 불규칙 변화를 하는 명사의 복수형을 써 보자.

1	a postman	ten	*postmen*
2	one fish	three	
3	a policeman	two	
4	a deer	nine	
5	one tooth	six	
6	a Chinese	seven	
7	a woman	four	
8	a child	five	
9	one ox	eight	
10	a sheep	two	
11	a foot	five	
12	one goose	ten	
13	people	three	
14	a mouse	six	
15	a Japanese	seven	

fish 생선
deer 사슴

다음은 명사의 복수형이다. 바르게 고쳐 써 보자.

toothbrush 칫솔
dragonfly 잠자리

	단수형	복수형		
1	a scarf	nine scarfes	→	*scarfs, scarves*
2	a foot	two foots	→	
3	a knife	five knifes	→	
4	a fish	two fishes	→	
5	a potato	three potatos	→	
6	a zoo	four zooes	→	
7	a toy	eight toies	→	
8	a child	seven childs	→	
9	a nurse	four nursees	→	
10	a toothbrush	teethbrush	→	
11	a dragonfly	dragonflys	→	
12	a mouse	six mouses	→	
13	a chief	three chieves	→	
14	a piano	nine pianoes	→	
15	a postman	seven postmans	→	

2

다음은 명사의 복수형이다. 바르게 고쳐 써 보자.

단수형	복수형		
1 a goose	two gooses	→	*geese*
2 a Japanese	six Japaneses	→	
3 a lady	ten ladys	→	
4 an ox	two oxes	→	
5 one wolf	six wolfes	→	
6 a deer	seven deers	→	
7 a tomato	four tomatos	→	
8 a glass	nine glassies	→	
9 a woman	four womans	→	
10 a country	three countrys	→	
11 a house	eight housees	→	
12 –	five peoples	→	
13 a sheep	nine sheeps	→	
14 a watch	six watchs	→	
15 a fox	three foxs	→	

Japanese 일본사람

[01–02] 다음 중 단수형과 복수형의 연결이 <u>잘못된</u> 것을 고르시오.

01
① foot - feet
② mouse - mice
③ woman - women
④ child - childs
⑤ goose - geese

01
불규칙 변화 복수형에 유의한다.

02
① piano - pianos
② potato - potatos
③ radio - radios
④ zoo - zoos
⑤ cello - cellos

03 다음 중 복수형을 만드는 방법이 <u>다른</u> 것은?

① lily
② party
③ butterfly
④ comedy
⑤ toy

04 다음은 복수형을 단수형으로 고친 것이다. 바르지 <u>않은</u> 것은?

① monkeys → monkey
② classmates → classmat
③ flies → fly
④ sportsmen → sportsman
⑤ sheep → sheep

05 다음 중 복수형을 만드는 방법이 <u>다른</u> 것은?

① knife
② leaf
③ wife
④ roof
⑤ thief

06 다음 빈칸에 들어갈 말이 순서대로 바르게 짝지어진 것은?

> I have one _____ , six _____ and two _____ .

① rulers - erasers - notebook
② ruler - erasers - notebooks
③ rulers - eraser - notebook
④ ruler - eraser - notebook
⑤ ruler - erasers - notebook

06
ruler 자
eraser 지우개
notebook 공책

실전Test

07 Tom이 동물원에 다녀와서 구경한 동물들을 다음과 같이 적어 보았다. 빈칸에 알맞은 말을 쓰시오.

- 두 마리의 여우 – two _____
- 세 마리의 사자 – three _____
- 다섯 마리의 사슴 – five _____

07

deer는 단수, 복수가 같은 형태이다.

08 다음 빈칸에 들어갈 말이 순서대로 바르게 짝지어진 것은?

- There are two _____ in this town.
- There are five _____ in my house.
- There are four _____ in the farm.

① churches - doors - ox
② churches - doors - oxen
③ church - door - oxen
④ church - doors - ox
⑤ churches - door - oxen

08

There are~ ~이 있다
church 교회
town 읍, 마을
farm 농장

[09-10] 다음 문장 중 바르지 <u>않은</u> 것을 고르시오.

 더알아보기

09
① I have one brothers.
② Five brushes are in the bag.
③ Paul has three nice cars.
④ Two cats are on the sofa.
⑤ They eat ten hamburgers.

09

hamburger 햄버거

10
① Five doctors are in the hospital.
② Two ladies are in the bank.
③ Ten peoples are in the plaza.
④ Ten postmen are in the post office.
⑤ Three skaters are in the ice rink.

10

hospital 병원
bank 은행
plaza 광장
skater 스케이트 타는
사람
ice rink 아이스링크

정답 및 해설 p.3

다음 빈칸에 알맞은 복수형 또는 단수형을 써 보자.

	단수형	복수형
1		trees
2	goose	
3	sheep	
4	chef	
5	monkey	
6		mice
7	ox	
8		lilies
9	eye	
10	photo	
11	postman	
12	deer	
13	Chinese	
14		leaves
15	box	

Unit 02

셀 수 없는 명사

셀 수 없는 명사는
양이 많고 적음을 나타낼 뿐,
명사 자체만으로는 복수형을 만들 수 없다.

Unit 02

셀 수 없는 명사

① 특징

셀 수 없는 명사는 양이 많고 적음을 나타낼 뿐, 명사 자체만으로는 복수형을 만들 수 없다.

즉, 명사 끝에 s나 es를 붙여 복수형을 만들 수 없다.

ex. butter~~s~~, coffee~~s~~, milk~~s~~, money~~s~~ …

② 종류

oil 기름
shampoo 샴푸
furniture 가구
gold 금
plastic 플라스틱
silver 은
soap 비누
air 공기
gas 가스
rice 쌀
history 역사
advice 충고
help 도움
information 정보
work 일

물질명사	형태가 없는 물질이나 재료를 나타내는 것	액체	oil, shampoo…
		고체	furniture, gold, plastic, silver, soap…
		기체	air, gas…
		음식	bread, butter, cheese, coffee, rice, tea, water…
추상명사	눈으로 보이지 않지만, 뜻으로 나타내는 것	과목	English, history, math, music, science…
		운동	baseball, basketball, golf, soccer, tennis…
		기타	advice, help, homework, information, mail, music, work…
고유명사	고유의 이름을 나타내는 것	사람	David, John, Mary, Jiho Park…
		도시	London, New York, Seoul…
		국가	America, China, Japan, Korea…

Tip! money는 셀 수 있는 명사처럼 느껴지지만, 영어에서는 셀 수 없는 명사로 취급하므로 주의한다.
ex. some money~~s~~ 약간의 돈   10 dollars 10 달러

수량 나타내기

셀 수 없는 명사는 담겨 있는 그릇이나 단위의 개수를 헤아림으로써 수량을 나타 낼 수 있다. 이를 조수사라고 하며, 조수사는 복수로 나타낼 수 있다.

ex. a cup of coffee 커피 한잔 **two cups of coffee** 커피 두 잔
　　 a loaf of bread 빵 한 덩어리 **two loaves of bread** 빵 두 덩어리

1 **셀 수 없는 명사의 수량 표시**

a **cup** of	water coffee tea	a **glass** of	water Coke juice milk
a **slice(piece)** of	bread cake cheese pizza	a **piece** of	advice furniture information music
a **sheet(piece)** of	paper blanket	a **bag** of	rice sugar
a **loaf** of	bread	a **tube** of	toothpaste
a **bottle** of	juice shampoo water	a **can** of	Coke corn
a **carton** of	juice, milk	a **bar** of	chocolate soap
a **jar** of	honey jam *pickles	a **bunch** of	*bananas *grapes

advice충고
furniture 가구
slice(piece) 조각
paper 종이
loaf 덩어리
bar 막대기
corn 옥수수
carton 판지로 만든
상자
tube 통, 관
toothpaste 치약
jar 병, 단지
bunch 다발, 송이

조수사 뒤에 pickle, banana, grape 등과 같이 셀 수 있는 명사가 올 때는 복수형을 쓴다.
ex. a jar of pickles 　　 a bunch of bananas

> **Tip!** · sheet는 보통 얇은 것 한 장을 의미하므로 종이나 담요 등을 표현할 때 사용한다.
> 　　　 *ex.* a sheet of blanket 담요 한 장
> 　　 · bunch는 동일한 것의 묶음을 말하며, 여러 종류의 것의 묶음은 bundle로 나타낸다.
> 　　　 *ex.* a bunch of roses 장미 한 다발 a bundle of flowers 꽃 한 다발
> 　　 · loaf의 복수형은 loaves이다.

다음 중 셀 수 <u>없는</u> 명사에 동그라미 해 보자.

kettle 주전자
oil 기름
rice 쌀
tray 쟁반

셀 수 없는 명사에는 액체,
음식, 보이지 않는 것 등이
있다.

1 bread

2 monkey

3 kettle

4 music

5 food

6 dress

7 money

8 country

9 oil

10 rice

11 roof

12 butter

13 tray

14 snow

15 shampoo

2

다음 중 셀 수 <u>없는</u> 명사에 동그라미 해 보자.

1 dog

2 chocolate

3 watch

4 cheese

5 gold

6 pepper

7 paper

8 sugar

9 church

10 key

11 furniture

12 fork

13 necklace

14 soap

15 baby

pepper 후추
furniture 가구
fork 포크
necklace 목걸이
soap 비누

다음 우리말에 맞도록 ( ) 안에서 알맞은 말을 골라 동그라미 해 보자.

loaf 덩어리
bottle 병
carton 판지로 만든 상자

1 물 2잔   two (cup, ⬭cups⬭) of (waters, ⬭water⬭)

2 빵 1덩어리   a (loaf, loaves) of (bread, breads)

3 바나나 2다발   two (bunches, bunch) of (banana, bananas)

4 쌀 4봉지   four (bags, bag) of (rices, rice)

5 샴푸 10통   ten (bottle, bottles) of (shampoo, shampoos)

6 우유 1팩   a (cartons, carton) of (milk, milks)

7 치약 5개   five (tubes, tube) of (toothpaste, toothpastes)

8 주스 3잔   three (glass, glasses) of (juices, juice)

9 가구 10점   ten (piece, pieces) of (furniture, furnitures)

10 피자 3조각   three (pieces, piece) of (pizzas, pizza)

11 빵 4조각   four (piece, pieces) of (bread, breads)

12 포도 6송이   six (bunches, bunch) of (grape, grapes)

13 비누 8개   eight (bar, bars) of (soaps, soap)

14 종이 1장   a (sheet, sheets) of (papers, paper)

15 피클 7병   seven (jar, jars) of (pickle, pickles)

4

다음 우리말에 맞도록 (   ) 안에서 알맞은 말을 골라 동그라미 해 보자.

1 잼 5병   five (bars, jars) of jam

2 콜라 2캔   two (cans, cups) of Coke.

3 꿀 6병   six (slices, jars) of honey

4 충고 한 마디   a (piece, carton) of advice

5 음악 한 곡   a (sheet, piece) of music

6 우유 2팩   two (bunches, cartons) of milk

7 가구 3점   three (bunches, pieces) of furniture.

8 초콜릿바 3개   three (bunches, bars) of chocolate

9 설탕 4봉지   four (bars, bags) of sugar

10 정보 한 가지   a (bar, piece) of information.

11 치즈 8조각   eight (pieces, loaves) of cheese

12 물 3병   three (bottles, slices) of water

13 주스 2팩   two (bunches, cartons) of juice

14 빵 7덩어리   seven (loaves, bars) of bread.

15 담요 1장   a (piece, loaf) of blanket

advice 충고
information 정보

14 빵 한 덩어리는
a loaf of bread
이지만 두 덩어리
이상은 loaf의 복수
형인 loaves를 쓴다.

다음 우리말에 맞도록 (   ) 안에서 알맞은 말을 골라 동그라미 해 보자.

furniture 가구
corn 옥수수
toothpaste 치약
carton 판지로 만든 상자

1 케이크 3조각   three (loaves, (pieces)) of cake

2 피자 9조각   nine (bars, pieces) of pizza

3 우유 5잔   five (glasses, bottles) of milk

4 가구 2점   two (sheets, pieces) of furniture

5 옥수수 4캔   four (cans, bottles) of corn

6 바나나 10다발   ten (bars, bunches) of (bananas, banana)

7 콜라 5잔   five (cans, glasses) of Coke

8 음악 2 곡   two (pieces, loaves) of music

9 주스 7병   seven (glasses, bottles) of juice

10 치약 3통   three (tubes, bars) of toothpaste

11 쌀 2봉지   two (bowls, bags) of rice

12 종이 6장   six (piece, sheets) of paper

13 충고 한 마디   a (piece, sheet) of advice

14 초콜릿바 8개   eight (bars, loaves) of chocolate

15 주스 2팩   two (cartons, glasses) of juice

6

다음 우리말에 맞도록 ( ) 안에서 알맞은 말을 골라 동그라미 해 보자.

1 콜라 5캔   five (cans, cartons) of Coke

2 세 가지 정보   three (pieces, sheets) of information

3 피클 7병   seven (loaves, jars) of pickles

4 콜라 3잔   three (glasses, cartons) of Coke

5 포도 8송이   eight (bowls, bunches) of grapes

6 비누 9개   nine (pieces, bars) of soap

7 차 7잔   seven (cups, glass) of tea

8 옥수수 통조림 6캔   six (bottles, cans) of (corn, corns)

9 가구 10점   ten (bars, pieces) of (furniture, furnitures)

10 우유 9팩   nine (cups, cartons) of milk

11 담요 3장   three (pieces, loaves) of blanket

12 설탕 7봉지   seven (bags, bottles) of sugar

13 치즈 5조각   five (sheets, pieces) of cheese

14 샴푸 8병   eight (cans, bottles) of shampoo

15 빵 4덩어리   four (loaves, pieces) of bread

advice 충고
tea 차

다음 빈칸에 우리말에 맞는 영어 표현을 써 보자.

1 바나나 3다발   three   *bunches*   of bananas

2 옥수수 2캔   two   of corn

3 비누 5개   five   of soap

4 우유 1팩   a   of milk

5 치즈 8조각   eight   of cheese

6 빵 3덩어리   three   of bread

7 세 가지 충고   three   of advice

8 커피 5잔   five   of coffee

9 쌀 3봉지   three   of rice

10 콜라 5캔   five   of Coke

11 치약 2개   two   of toothpaste

12 포도 7송이   seven   of grapes

13 주스 2팩   two   of juice

14 음악 3곡   three   of music

15 정보 두 가지   two   of information

2

다음 빈칸에 우리말에 맞는 영어 표현을 써 보자.

1 우유 2팩   two   *cartons*   of milk

2 물 6병   six   of water

3 초콜릿바 2개   two   of chocolate

4 종이 4장   four   of paper

5 주스 9병   nine   of juice

6 빵 8조각   eight   of bread

7 가구 3점   three   of furniture

8 밀가루 7봉지   seven   of flour

9 차 3잔   three   of tea

10 피클 5병   five   of pickles

11 정보 3가지   three   of information

12 케이크 2조각   two   of cake

13 샴푸 2통   two   of shampoo

14 옥수수 6캔   six   of corn

15 피자 8조각   eight   of pizza

flour 밀가루

다음 밑줄 친 부분들 중에서 **틀린** 곳을 바르게 고쳐 써 보자.

1 two cups of teas
   tea

2 two jars of pickle

3 three loaf of bread

4 a cans of corn

5 ten bunches of banana

6 seven glass of milk

7 eight bottles of shampoos

8 two bottle of juice

9 six loaves of pizza

10 nine bunches of furniture

11 three pieces of musics

12 four bunches of grape

13 four jars of soap

14 five bags of rices

15 a sheet of papers

2

다음 밑줄 친 부분들 중에서 틀린 곳을 바르게 고쳐 써 보자.

1 two <u>bunches</u> of <u>pickles</u>
jars

2 three <u>glass</u> of <u>Coke</u>

3 seven <u>cans</u> of <u>shampoo</u>

4 two <u>piece</u> of <u>pizza</u>

5 four <u>pieces</u> of <u>cheeses</u>

6 six <u>bunch</u> of <u>grapes</u>

7 a <u>piece</u> of <u>sugar</u>

8 eight <u>tubes</u> of <u>honey</u>

9 a <u>cans</u> of <u>corn</u>

10 seven <u>bars</u> of <u>toothpaste</u>

11 two <u>slices</u> of <u>blanket</u>

12 a <u>piece</u> of <u>informations</u>

13 three <u>cartons</u> of <u>bananas</u>

14 a <u>pieces</u> of <u>cake</u>

15 a <u>tube</u> of <u>chocolate</u>

01 다음 중 셀 수 있는 명사는?

① gold
② help
③ dress
④ information
⑤ salt

02 다음 중 밑줄 친 부분이 올바른 것은?

① I have some <u>food</u>.
② You have some <u>soups</u>.
③ I have some <u>oils</u>.
④ You need some <u>waters</u>.
⑤ I have some <u>sugars</u>.

02

need 필요하다

셀 수 없는 명사는 복수형
으로 쓸 수 없다.

[03-04] 다음 중 바르지 <u>않은</u> 것을 고르시오.

03
① a cup of tea
② a glass of juice
③ a bunch of cake
④ a bottle of shampoo
⑤ a bag of rice

정답 및 해설 p.5

04
① six can of corn
② a jar of pickles
③ five sheets of paper
④ a piece of information
⑤ two cups of tea

05 다음 빈칸에 들어갈 말로 알맞지 <u>않은</u> 것은?

I have a piece of _____ .

① bread   ② advice
③ furniture   ④ cheese
⑤ rice

06 다음 우리말에 맞도록 빈칸에 알맞은 말을 쓰시오.

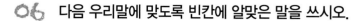

> 나의 남동생은 빵 세 덩어리를 먹는다.
>
> → My brother eats three _____ of bread.

07 다음 빈칸에 알맞은 말을 쓰시오.

> • a _____ of soap
>
> • two _____ of toothpaste
>
> • three _____ of bananas

08 다음 밑줄 친 것 중 바르지 않은 것은?

> My face is round. I have ① two brown eyes and
> ② small ears. I have ③ a big nose. I have ④ long arms
> and short legs. I have ⑤ brown hairs.

08

round 둥근

셀 수 없는 명사와 셀 수 있는 명사를 구분한다.

[09-10] 다음 글을 읽고, 물음에 답하시오.

> I go to the ABC market everyday. I buy _____ milk.
>
> And I come back home. I drink _____ milk.
>
> I eat ⓐ two piece of cheese and _____ grapes.

09 위 글의 빈칸에 들어갈 말을 골라 순서대로 번호를 쓰시오.

> ① a bunch of ② a glass of ③ a carton of

_____ _____ _____

10 위 글의 밑줄 친 ⓐ에서 틀린 부분을 찾아 바르게 고쳐 쓰시오.

_____ ⇨ _____

Quiz!

우리말에 맞도록 빈칸을 채워 보자.

1	주스 3잔	three	of juice
2	가구 1점	a	of furniture
3	종이 2장	two	of paper
4	빵 4덩어리	four	of bread
5	쌀 2봉지	two	of rice
6	비누 1개	a	of soap
7	충고 한 마디	a	of advice
8	샴푸 1통	a	of shampoo
9	옥수수 2캔	two	of corn
10	바나나 3다발	three	of bananas
11	우유 4팩	four	of milk
12	치약 3개	three	of toothpaste
13	피클 5병	five	of pickles
14	포도 2송이	two	of grapes
15	정보 한 편	a	of information

Unit 03

관사

명사 앞에 붙어서
막연한 것을 나타낼 때는 부정관사 a(an)을,
명백한 것을 나타낼 때는 정관사 the를 쓴다.

Unit 03 관사

관사란?

명사 앞에 붙어 그 명사의 의미를 한정하거나 제한하며, 부정관사와 정관사가 있다.

❶ 부정관사 a (an)

a나 an은 「하나의, 어떤~」의 의미로 해석하기도 하고 굳이 해석하지 않기도 한다.

① a (an)을 붙이는 경우

❶ 자음으로 시작하는 단수 명사 앞에는 a, 모음으로 시작하는 단수 명사 앞에는 an을 붙인다.	a boy, a girl… an egg, an apple…
❷ 명사가 자음으로 시작할지라도 명사를 꾸며주는 형용사가 모음으로 시작할 때는 an을 붙인다.	an old clock an easy book…
❸ 명사가 모음으로 시작할지라도 명사를 꾸며주는 형용사가 자음으로 시작할 때는 a를 붙인다.	an egg a fresh egg
❹ 자음으로 시작하지만 모음 소리가 나는 명사 앞에 an을 붙여준다.	~a~ hour → an hour ~a~ honest boy → an honest boy
❺ 모음으로 시작하지만 발음이 [j], [w] 인 경우 a를 붙여준다.	~an~ university → a university ~an~ European → a European

> **Tip!** a(an)는 명사가 정해지지 않았다는 의미를 나타내어 부정(不定)관사, the는 정해져 있다는 의미를 나타내어 정(定)관사라 한다.

> **Tip!** hour나 honest의 경우, h는 자음이지만 소리나지 않는 묵음이므로 o를 단어의 첫 글자로 생각하여 an을 붙여준다.

② a (an)을 붙이지 못하는 경우

❶ 복수명사 앞에	~a~ dogs, ~a~ watches…
❷ 고유명사 앞에	~a~ Korea, ~an~ America…
❸ 셀 수 없는 명사 앞에	~a~ milk, ~a~ bread…
❹ 소유격 앞에	~a~ my book, ~a~ your pen…

정관사 the

고유명사 이외의 명사 앞에 붙어 그 명사가 특정한 것임을 나타낸다.

a(an)	하나의, 어떤	정해지지 않은 불특정 명사 앞에 붙는다
the	그	이미 정해진 특정 명사 앞에 붙는다.

ex. I buy an apple. 나는 사과 하나를 산다. (정해지지 않은 사과)
The apple is green. 그 사과는 초록색이다. (이미 정해진 사과)

 정관사 the를 붙이는 경우와 붙이지 않는 경우

① **정관사 the를 붙이는 경우**

세상에 하나 밖에 없는 자연물 앞에	위치, 방향 앞에	연주하는 악기 이름 앞에	호텔, 식당, 극장, 박물관 이름 앞에	강, 바다 이름 앞에
the sky the sun the earth the world···	the right the top the end the east···	the piano the cello the violin the flute···	the Hilton hotel the Bennigan's the British Museum	the Nile the East Sea

earth 지구
world 세계
end 마지막
right 오른쪽
top 꼭대기
east 동쪽
British Museum
대영박물관
Wall Street 월가
Incheon International
airport 인천 국제 공항
Seoul Station 서울역
Havard University
하버드 대학교

② **정관사 the를 붙이지 않는 경우**

식사 이름 앞에	운동 이름 앞에	교통수단 앞에	거리, 공항, 역, 대학 이름 앞에
breakfast lunch supper dinner	tennis soccer football baseball···	by bus by taxi by train on foot···	Wall Street Incheon International airport Seoul Station Havard University

Tip! 아침에 학교에 가려면 식사를 빨리 해야한다. 식사를 빨리 하려면 식사 앞에 the 같은 것이 있으면 시간이 더 걸린다. 그래서 식사 앞에는 the가 있으면 곤란하다.

Tip! 자연물 앞에는 the를 붙이고, 인공물 앞에는 the를 붙이지 않는다고 생각하면 쉽다. 단, 인공물 중에 먹고(식당), 자고(호텔), 구경하는(극장, 박물관) 것, 연주하는 악기 앞에만 the를 붙인다라고 생각하고 외우면 쉽다.
→ 더(the) 먹(고) 자(고) 구(경하고) 악(기)

③ **습관적인 the의 사용 유무**

watch video, listen to music, listen to **the** radio 등이 있다.

다음 (   ) 안에서 알맞은 관사를 골라 보자.

green 초록색의
beautiful 아름다운

1 (ⓐ, an, ×) desk

2 (a, an, ×) desks

3 (a, an, ×) old desks

4 (a, an, ×) your desk

5 (a, an, ×) old desk

6 (a, an, ×) my houses

7 (a, an, ×) green house

8 (a, an, ×) my green house

9 (a, an, ×) green houses

10 (a, an, ×) very big green house

11 (a, an, ×) very beautiful roses

12 (a, an, ×) rose

13 (a, an, ×) beautiful rose

14 (a, an, ×) her beautiful roses

15 (a, an, ×) very beautiful rose

다음 (   ) 안에서 알맞은 관사를 골라 보자.

1 (a, an, ⊗) his children

2 (a, an, ×) honest child

3 (a, an, ×) children

4 (a, an, ×) honest children

5 (a, an, ×) child

6 (a, an, ×) Tom's honest children

7 (a, an, ×) tomato

8 (a, an, ×) red tomatoes

9 (a, an, ×) Jane's tomatoes

10 (a, an, ×) Jane's tomato

11 (a, an, ×) red tomato

12 (a, an, ×) very red tomatoes

13 (a, an, ×) very red tomato

14 (a, an, ×) Jane's red tomatoes

15 (a, an, ×) tomatoes

다음 빈칸에 a나 an을 쓰거나, 필요 없는 곳에 ×표를 해 보자.

angel 천사
France 프랑스
pot 단지, 냄비
brush 솔
vase 꽃병
coach 코치
ant 개미

1	*a* map	2	orange
3	buses	4	watches
5	egg	6	hair
7	my book	8	potato
9	bird	10	truck
11	Korea	12	notebooks
13	money	14	angel
15	ball	16	France
17	pots	18	work
19	brushes	20	sugar
21	apple	22	Tom
23	his car	24	CD
25	Jane	26	shirts
27	my mother's vase	28	her coach
29	coffee	30	ant

4

다음 빈칸에 a나 an을 쓰거나, 필요 **없는** 곳에 ×표를 해 보자.

1	× Paris	2		chairs
3	her ring	4		salt
5	money	6		actor
7	pens	8		homework
9	America	10		my car
11	university	12		room
13	butter	14		Europe
15	picture	16		dragonfly
17	airplane	18		ice cream
19	designer	20		China
21	hour	22		kites
23	melons	24		his watch
25	our house	26		Mr. Brown
27	countries	28		juice
29	elephant	30		lily

actor 남자배우
university 대학
Europe 유럽
dragonfly 잠자리
designer 디자이너
hour 시간
China 중국
kite 연

다음 빈칸에 the가 필요하면 the를, 필요하지 않으면 ×를 골라 보자.

Amazon 아마존강
west 서쪽
Hilton hotel 힐튼 호텔

1 play (the, ×) tennis

2 play (the, ×) piano

3 (the, ×) sun

4 (the, ×) Amazon

5 (the, ×) west

6 (the, ×) left

7 (the, ×) sky

8 have (the, ×) dinner

9 play (the, ×) cello

10 play (the, ×) baseball

11 (the, ×) East Sea

12 (the, ×) top

13 (the, ×) earth

14 have (the, ×) lunch

15 (the, ×) Hilton hotel

6

다음 빈칸에 the가 필요하면 the를, 필요하지 않으면 ×를 골라 보자.

1 (the , ×) Bennigan's

2 (the , ×) north

3 play ((the , ×) basketball

4 eat ((the , ×) breakfast

5 (the , ×) right

6 play (the , ×) violin

7 (the , ×) east

8 (the , ×) middle

9 (the , ×) Park Ji-seong Street Park Ji-seong Street 박지성길

10 (the , ×) Busan Station

11 (the , ×) moon

12 (the , ×) Nile

13 (the , ×) Palace hotel

14 (the , ×) Harvard University

15 (the , ×) Kennedy airport

north 북쪽
middle 가운데
street 길
station 역
moon 달
Palace hotel 팰리스 호텔
Kennedy airport
케네디 공항

다음 빈칸에 a(an)나 the를 쓰거나, 필요 <u>없는</u> 곳에 ×표를 해 보자.

right food 좋은 식품
look like ~처럼 보이다
Leuvre Museum
루브르 박물관
bus driver 버스 운전 기사
puppy 강아지
expensive 값비싼
bracelet 팔찌
clean 깨끗한
here 여기
Russia 러시아
eggplant 가지
sixty minutes 60분

1 부정관사 a, an은 셀 수 있는 단수명사 앞에만 붙는다. 복수명사, 셀 수 없는 명사, 형용사 (뒤에 명사없이 형용사만 오는 경우) 앞에는 붙지 않는다.

1 ____×____ milk is right food.

2 He is _____ policeman.

3 She looks like _____ angel.

4 We visit _____ Louvre Museum.

5 He is _____ bus driver.

6 They are _____ bus drivers.

7 _____ sugar is sweet.

8 It is _____ his puppy. _____ puppy is white.

9 The men are _____ kind teachers.

10 They are _____ albums.

11 That is _____ expensive bracelet.

12 These are _____ clean houses.

13 Here is _____ Russia.

14 This is _____ eggplant.

15 _____ hour has sixty minutes.

2

다음 빈칸에 a(an)나 the를 쓰거나, 필요 없는 곳에 ×표를 해 보자.

stamp 우표
worth 가치가 있는
sour 신맛의
interesting 흥미로운
cook 요리사
peel 껍질을 벗기다
be chopped 다져지다
actor 남자 배우
Outback Steakhouse
아웃백 스테이크하우스

1 Jane is *a* happy woman.

2 Those are   her stamps.   stamps are very worth.

3 It is   old car.

4 We are on   Wall Street.

5 Tulips are   flowers.

6 That is   my son's horse.

7 There is   university in this town.

8   juice is sour.

9 Those are   interesting stories.

10 You have   new watch.

11 She is   cook.

12 Mom peels   onion.   onion is chopped.

13   James wants to be   actor.

14 Tom stays at   Hyatt hotel.

15 We have dinner in   Outback Steakhouse.

다음 빈칸에 a(an)나 the를 쓰거나, 필요 <u>없는</u> 곳에 ×표를 해 보자.

cashier 계산원
ugly 못생긴
dolphin 돌고래
animal 동물
cucumber 오이
favorite 마음에 드는
subject 과목
among ~중에서, ~가운데
excellent 우수한
computer programmer
컴퓨터 프로그래머
carrot 당근
refrigerator 냉장고

1 Mary is   *a*   very kind cashier.

2 This is   ugly doll.

3 It is   cold day today.

4 A dolphin is cute.   animal is very smart.

5 It is   her cucumber.

6 A lot of buildings are here.   buildings are high.

7 I go to   Kimpo airport.

8   math is   my favorite subject.

9   bee is among the roses.   bee is very big.

10 I sometimes watch   video.

11 They are   very excellent computer programmers.

12 There is   carrot in the refrigerator.

13   Mrs. Park is   my aunt.

14 She lives in   L.A.

15   John is   honest boy.

4

다음 빈칸에 a(an)나 the를 쓰거나, 필요 없는 곳에 ×표를 해 보자.

1 We live on *the* earth.

2 She listens to   music.

3 I have   friend.   friend is very handsome.

4 He sails on   Yellow Sea.

5 They have   dinner at 6.

6   Han river is very wide and long.

7   sun rises in   east.

8   earth moves around   sun.

9 She plays   tennis.

10 We go to   Seoul University.

11 I have   umbrella.   umbrella is Matt's.

12   moon is round.

13 Sumi and I walk to   top.

14 Tom plays   soccer with his friends.

15 I like to listen to   radio.

sail 항해하다
Yellow Sea 황해
wide 넓은
rise 뜨다, 오르다
move 움직이다
around ~ 주위에
round 둥근

3, 11
앞에 나온 특정 명사를
다시 언급할 경우,
그 명사 앞에 the를
붙인다.
ex. There is a girl.
소녀가 한 명 있다.
The girl(She) is my
sister.
그 소녀는(그녀는)
내 여동생이다.

다음 밑줄 친 부분들 중에서 틀린 곳을 바르게 고쳐 써 보자.

barber 이발사
Japan 일본
actress 여배우
puppy 강아지
European 유럽사람
gas station 주유소
dish 접시
pumpkin 호박
shopkeeper 가게 주인

1 He is a good barbers.
              barber

2 I want to go to a Japan.

3 She is a actress.

4 They are a puppies.

5 Robbin is an European.

6 The gas station is a large.

7 My mother has a big dish. A dish is my grandmother's.

8 This is a my sister's red coat.

9 It is an university.

10 Those are a nice airplanes.

11 He buys two pumpkin.

12 You eat some cheese. A cheese smells sweet.

13 Mr. Brown is a old man.

14 He is a honest shopkeeper.

15 That is an oxen.

2

다음 밑줄 친 부분들 중에서 **틀린** 곳을 바르게 고쳐 써 보자.

1 Eat the breakfast at 7 o'clock.
 ✕

2 Judy is in middle of the bus.

3 Turn to right and go straight.

4 They play the baseball after school.

5 The Kennedy airport is very large.

6 Many people are in the Seoul Station.

7 She is at end of the line.

8 I buy a melon. A melon is yellow.

9 We listen to the music everyday.

10 An universe is endless.

11 She looks at top of the tower.

12 My son has a violin. A violin is very expensive.

13 I watch the video.

14 Shilla Hotel is in Seoul.

15 There are sixty minutes in a hour.

실전Test

01 다음 빈칸에 들어갈 말로 알맞지 <u>않은</u> 것은?

> This is a _____.

① eggplant   ② mailbox

③ tulip   ④ computer

⑤ dragonfly

02 다음 빈칸에 들어갈 말이 순서대로 바르게 짝지어진 것은?

> · He is _____ honest man.
>
> · This is _____ fresh egg.

① a – an   ② an – an

③ a – a   ④ an – a

⑤ an – 필요없음

03 다음 중 빈칸에 a가 들어갈 수 <u>없는</u> 것은? (2개)

① Tom is _____ student.

② This is _____ my new bag.

③ That is _____ sweet apple.

④ It is _____ very nice car.

⑤ _____ sun is in the sky.

04 다음 중 밑줄 친 the가 바르게 쓰인 것은?

① My family have <u>the</u> lunch.
② Jack plays <u>the</u> soccer after school.
③ This is <u>the</u> Japan.
④ I play <u>the</u> flute everyday.
⑤ Rosa goes to <u>the</u> Incheon Airport.

04

family 가족
after school 방과 후에
Japan 일본
airport 공항

05 다음 문장 중 바르지 <u>않은</u> 것 두 개를 고르면?

① It is a big elephant.
② My sister and I are a singer.
③ They are a wise women.
④ The moon is beautiful.
⑤ That is an igloo.

05

igloo 얼음집

06 다음 중 관사의 사용이 <u>잘못된</u> 것은?

① a boy
② a hour
③ a desk
④ an actor
⑤ an ice cream

06

hour 시간
actor 배우

정답 및 해설 p.6, 7

07 다음 빈칸에 들어갈 말이 순서대로 바르게 짝지어진 것은?

> I see _____ snake. _____ snake is very long.

① a - An
② the - An
③ a - The
④ an - The
⑤ a - 필요없음

08 다음 중 밑줄 친 부분의 쓰임이 옳은 것은?

① I am <u>a</u> Kim Minho.
② That is <u>a</u> expensive ring.
③ It is <u>an</u> interesting story.
④ The girl is <u>a</u> very pretty.
⑤ He has <u>a</u> dinner.

07

snake 뱀

헷갈리는 정관사 the!
아래와 같이 기억해 두자.
• 학교에 지각하지 않으려면 식사를 빨리 해야 하는데 the 같은 것이 발에 걸리면 시간이 더 걸릴 것이다. 그래서 식사 앞에는 the를 붙이지 않는다.

• 운동 경기할 때도 빨리 빨리 공을 차야 하는데 the가 가로막고 있으면 골치 아프겠지?
그래서 운동 경기 앞에는 the를 붙이지 않는다.

• 악기는 박자를 정확히 맞춰 연주해야 하니까 매트로놈(박자 맞추는 기구)에 해당하는 the가 꼭 있어야 한다고 생각하고 외우자.

09 다음 빈칸에 공통으로 들어갈 말로 알맞은 것은?

> · Mary is in _____ middle of the bus.
>
> · The flower shop is at _____ end of the street.

① a
② an
③ the
④ one
⑤ 필요없음

09
middle 중간, 중앙
end 끝, 마지막

정답 및 해설 p.6, 7

10 다음 문장에서 틀린 부분을 바르게 고쳐 쓰시오.

> A sugar is sweet.

_____ ⇨ _____

다음 빈칸에 a(an)나 the를 쓰거나, 필요 없는 곳에 ×표를 해 보자.

1 I have _____ breakfast.

2 They play _____ flute.

3 He goes to _____ Yale University.

4 We need _____ umbrella.

5 The boys play _____ soccer.

6 I see _____ moon with my friend.

7 _____ sun sets in _____ west.

8 My mother gives me a book. _____ book is popular.

9 That is _____ British Museum.

10 English is _____ my favorite subject.

11 She is in _____ middle of the bus.

12 I know _____ honest man. _____ man is Jim's friend.

13 We go to _____ Daegu Station.

14 Look at _____ sky!

15 We have a good time at _____ Bennigan's.

| Yale University |
| 예일대학교 |
| moon 달 |
| set 지다 |
| popular 인기있는 |
| British Museum |
| 대영박물관 |
| favorite 가장 좋아하는 |
| subject 과목 |
| Daegu Station 대구역 |

Unit 04

인칭대명사와
지시대명사

대명사는 명사 대신 쓰는 말이다.
인칭대명사는 사람을 대신하는 대명사이고,
지시대명사는 사물을 대신하는 대명사이다.

인칭대명사와 지시대명사

대명사란?

의미 명사를 대신해서 쓰는 말이다.

종류 ❶ 인칭대명사 : 사람을 가리키는 대명사

ex. I 나, you 너, he 그, she 그녀, it 그것, they 그들

❷ 지시대명사 : 사물을 가리키는 대명사

ex. this 이것, that 저것, these 이것들, those 저것들

> **Tip!** 그 외에도 소유대명사(mine, yours 등), 의문대명사(what, who 등), 부정대명사(one 등), 관계대명사(who, which 등) 등이 있다.

1 인칭대명사

1 인칭의 구별

1인칭	나	말하는 사람
2인칭	너 (당신)	말을 듣는 상대방
3인칭	나와 너를 뺀 나머지 모두	그 이외의 나머지 모두

2 인칭대명사의 종류

	단수	복수
1인칭	I 나는	we 우리들은
2인칭	you 너는	you 너희들은
3인칭	he 그는, she 그녀는, it 그것은	they 그들은 / 그녀들은 / 그것들은

ex. I am a singer. 나는 가수입니다.

She is my teacher. 그녀는 나의 선생님입니다.

We are singers. 우리들은 가수입니다.

They are erasers. 그것들은 지우개입니다.

지시대명사

사물이나 장소를 가리키는 대명사로, 3인칭에 해당한다.

1 지시대명사의 종류

	단수	복수
가까운 것을 가리킬 때	this	these
멀리 있는 것을 가리킬 때	that	those

ex. This is a ball.   이것은 공이다.   These are balls.   이것들은 공(들)이다.

That is a ball.   저것은 공이다.   Those are balls.   저것들은 공(들)이다.

 That is a ball.

 Those are balls.

 This is a ball.

 These are balls.

 주어와 보어

주어가 단수이면 보어도 단수/셀 수 없는 명사를 쓰고, 주어가 복수이면 보어도 복수를 쓴다.

ex. **She is a student.**   ~~She is students.~~
주어(단수)   보어(단수)

They are students.   ~~They are a student.~~
주어(복수)   보어(복수)

This is hot water.   ~~These are waters.~~
주어(단수)   보어(셀 수 없는 명사)

지시대명사가 사람을 나타낼 때도 있다.

ex. **This is Inho.**   이 사람은 인호입니다.

> **Tip!** 인칭대명사와 be동사
> 인칭대명사의 인칭과 수에 따라 am, are, is로 be동사를 구별하여 쓴다.

 **주어와 보어**

> • 주어 : 문장의 주인이라고 생각하면 된다. 동작을 행하는 주체로서 우리말에서는 「~은, ~는, ~이, ~가」에 해당한다. 주로 명사, 대명사가 주어의 위치에 온다.
> • 보어 : 주어를 보충 설명해 주는 말이다. (목적어를 보충 설명하기도 한다.) 명사나 형용사가 보어의 위치에 온다.

주어진 대명사의 복수형을 써 보자.

1 you   *you*

2 he

3 I

4 that

5 she

6 this

7 it

주어진 대명사의 단수형을 써 보자.

1 these   *this*

2 you(너희들은)

3 they(그들은)

4 they(그것들은)

5 we

6 those

7 they(그녀들은)

2

다음 ( ) 안에 인칭과 단수, 복수를 골라 동그라미 해 보자.

1	they	(1, 2, ③) 인칭	(단수, 복수)	

face 얼굴

1   they   (1, 2, ③) 인칭   (단수, 복수)

2   my hand   (1, 2, 3) 인칭   (단수, 복수)

3   I   (1, 2, 3) 인칭   (단수, 복수)

4   Joe and Judy   (1, 2, 3) 인칭   (단수, 복수)

5   she   (1, 2, 3) 인칭   (단수, 복수)

6   your face   (1, 2, 3) 인칭   (단수, 복수)

7   we   (1, 2, 3) 인칭   (단수, 복수)

8   you (너희들은)   (1, 2, 3) 인칭   (단수, 복수)

9   our friends   (1, 2, 3) 인칭   (단수, 복수)

10 the cats   (1, 2, 3) 인칭   (단수, 복수)

11 he   (1, 2, 3) 인칭   (단수, 복수)

12 he and she   (1, 2, 3) 인칭   (단수, 복수)

13 Korea   (1, 2, 3) 인칭   (단수, 복수)

14 my sisters   (1, 2, 3) 인칭   (단수, 복수)

15 you (너)   (1, 2, 3) 인칭   (단수, 복수)

다음 빈칸에 인칭을 표시하고, 단수인지 복수인지 써 보자.

Mozart 모차르트
donut 도넛
puppy 강아지
grandmother 할머니
its 그것의
ear 귀
Busan 부산
our 우리들의
class 수업
tulip 튤립

1 Mozart   *3* 인칭   단 수

2 I   인칭   수

3 the donuts   인칭   수

4 Jane and Bill   인칭   수

5 we   인칭   수

6 her puppy   인칭   수

7 my hats   인칭   수

8 your grandmother   인칭   수

9 you (너희들은)   인칭   수

10 its ears   인칭   수

11 Busan   인칭   수

12 it   인칭   수

13 our classes   인칭   수

14 you (너는)   인칭   수

15 tulips   인칭   수

4

다음 ( ) 안에서 알맞은 말을 골라 동그라미 해 보자.

1 (I, we) am a cashier.

2 (This, These) is hot tea.

3 (That, Those) are Tom's shirts.

4 (You, He) are good parents.

5 (It, They) is a cello.

6 (It, They) are Mr. Kim's sons.

7 (This, These) is a rabbit.

8 (It, They) are potatoes.

9 (That, Those) is my watch.

10 (We, I) are students.

11 (You, We) are a teacher.

12 (This, These) are bees.

13 (Tom, Tom and Judy) is an artist.

14 (Tom, Tom and Judy) are teachers.

15 (That, Those) is delicious cheese.

cashier 계산원
tea 차
parents 부모님
rabbit 토끼
potato 감자
watch 손목시계
bee 벌
artist 예술가
delicious 맛있는

다음 (   ) 안에서 알맞은 말을 골라 동그라미 해 보자.

duck 오리
credit card 신용카드
celebrity 연예인
worm 벌레
painter 화가
clothing store 옷 가게
baseball player 야구 선수
teller 은행 출납원

1 (This, These) are ducks.

2 (I, We) am a doctor.

3 (They, It) are children.

4 (It, They) is a credit card.

5 (John, John and Tom) are celebrities.

6 (I, We) are old ladies.

7 (This, These) is a tomato.

8 (That, Those) are worms.

9 (The man, The men) are painters.

10 (They, She) is my aunt.

11 (It, They) is a clothing store.

12 (You, She) are nice baseball players.

13 (It, They) are small mice.

14 (Seoul, Seoul and Busan) are big cities.

15 (She, They) is a teller.

6

다음 (   ) 안에서 알맞은 말을 골라 동그라미 해 보자.

1 It is (a fly, flies).

2 They are (a fly, flies).

3 She is (a shopkeeper, shopkeepers).

4 I am (a farmer, farmers).

5 They are (her cousin, her cousins).

6 Those are (my sunflower, my sunflowers).

7 (He, She and he) is a golfer.

8 It is cold (juice, juices).

9 They are too young (a soldier, soldiers).

10 That is (a blue diamond, blue diamonds)

11 They are (a melon, melons).

12 We are (his daughter, his daughters).

13 That is warm (bread, breads).

14 This is (a ticket, tickets) for you.

15 These are (my notebook, my notebooks).

shopkeeper 가게 주인
cousin 사촌
sunflower 해바라기
golfer 골프 선수
too young 너무 어린
soldier 군인
diamond 다이아몬드
melon 참외
ticket 표

다음 빈칸에 ( ) 안의 대명사를 알맞은 형태로 고쳐 써 보자.

pillow 베개
sweet 달콤한
hairdresser 미용사
guitarist 기타연주자
postcard 우편엽서
businessman 사업가
blanket 담요
actress 여배우
giraffe 기린
hungry 배고픈
fox 여우
fragrant 향기로운

1   *This*   is an ice cream. (this)

2 _____ are Jane's brothers. (he)

3 _____ are soft pillows. (that)

4 _____ is sweet jam. (this)

5 _____ are hairdressers. (I)

6 _____ are a wonderful guitarist. (you)

7 _____ is a postcard. (that)

8 _____ are businessmen. (he)

9 _____ are white blankets. (that)

10 _____ is an actress. (she)

11 _____ is Susan's brother. (this)

12 _____ are giraffes. (this)

13 _____ are his students. (you)

14 _____ are hungry foxes. (It)

15 _____ is fragrant shampoo. (it)

2

다음 빈칸에 ( ) 안의 대명사를 알맞은 형태로 고쳐 써 보자.

1	*They*	are clocks. (it)	
2		is brown sugar. (this)	
3		are deer. (that)	
4		is a worker. (he)	
5		is a wonderful scarf. (it)	
6		are sharp knives. (this)	
7		is a green bean. (it)	
8		are boxers. (I)	
9		are old violins. (this)	
10		are a great designer. (you)	
11		is Tom's nephew. (he)	
12		are your keys. (that)	
13		are my students. (he)	
14		are lilies. (it)	
15		are famous musicians. (she)	

bean 콩
boxer 권투 선수
designer 디자이너
nephew (남자)조카
musician 음악가

다음 빈칸에 (   ) 안의 대명사를 알맞은 형태로 고쳐 써 보자.

cellphone 휴대 전화
yours 너의 것
excellent 유능한
pilot 조종사
mine 나의 것
cook 요리사
famous 유명한
skater 스케이트 선수
fire fighter 소방관

1 _They_ are new cell phones. (It)

2 _____ are yours. (this)

3 _____ is an excellent pilot. (he)

4 _____ are mine. (that)

5 _____ are cooks. (I)

6 _____ is Judy's banana. (this)

7 _____ are kind nurses. (she)

8 _____ are old men. (you)

9 _____ is a fork. (it)

10 _____ are Tom's game CDs. (that)

11 _____ are wonderful dresses. (this)

12 _____ is a toy. (that)

13 _____ are pretty dolls. (this)

14 _____ is a famous skater. (she)

15 _____ are fire fighters. (he)

다음 빈칸에 (   ) 안의 명사를 알맞은 형태로 고쳐 써 보자.

1 We are   *coaches*   . (coach)

2 He is an   . (engineer)

3 Those are fast   . (train)

4 Those are   . (coin)

5 These are your   . (car)

6 That is a poor   . (wolf)

7 It is a strong   . (bull)

8 She is his   . (daughter)

9 They are   . (tiger)

10 My brothers are   . (photographer)

11 This is a locked   . (box)

12 They are small   . (potato)

13 Those are   . (scientist)

14 You (너희들은) are diligent   . (postman)

15 Mary and Jane are my   . (sister)

engineer 기술자
coin 동전
poor 불쌍한
bull 황소
daughter 딸
photographer 사진사
locked 잠긴
scientist 과학자
diligent 부지런한
postman 우편집배원

다음 밑줄 친 부분들 중에서 **틀린** 곳을 바르게 고쳐 써 보자.

vest 조끼
cane 지팡이
excellent 유능한
boxer 권투 선수
restaurant 식당
artist 예술가
pet 애완 동물
kiwi 키위

1 You (너희들은) are good violinist.
  violinists

2 It is your vests.

3 The girl are Sumi's sisters.

4 This is his canes.

5 Judy and Ann are excellent doctor.

6 Those are pink rose.

7 You (너는) are a tennis players.

8 They is a yellow boat.

9 Nancy is his good wives.

10 The young men is a boxer.

11 These is a very nice restaurant.

12 She looks like an artists.

13 The dogs is my pet.

14 These are small kiwi.

15 They is a happy girl.

2

다음 밑줄 친 부분들 중에서 **틀린** 곳을 바르게 고쳐 써 보자.

1 I am a <u>healthy</u> <u>women</u>.
  woman

2 Mr. Williams is a <u>nice</u> <u>guys</u>.

3 They <u>are</u> horror <u>movie</u>.

4 She is <u>my</u> <u>nieces</u>.

5 The <u>kings</u> is a <u>wise</u> man.

6 These <u>are</u> special <u>ring</u> for me.

7 The <u>little</u> <u>boys</u> is a singer.

8 <u>Ann</u> is a skinny <u>girls</u>.

9 <u>It</u> are <u>diligent</u> bees.

10 The <u>teacher</u> are <u>great</u> pianists.

11 <u>Those</u> is a <u>fantastic</u> hamburger.

12 Jim <u>and</u> Tom are <u>fisherman</u>.

13 Lions and crocodiles are <u>wild</u> <u>animal</u>.

14 She is a <u>pretty</u> and kind <u>ladies</u>.

15 <u>My</u> boss is a <u>gentlemen</u>.

healthy 건강한
guy 사람, 남자
horror 무서운
movie 영화
niece (여자)조카
wise 현명한
special 특별한
skinny 마른
diligent 근면한
bee 벌
fantastic 환상적인
fisherman 어부
animal 동물
gentleman 신사

01 다음 중 인칭과 단수, 복수를 바르게 나타낸 것은?

① my mother - 1인칭 단수
② his computers - 3인칭 단수
③ our class - 3인칭 복수
④ your hands - 2인칭 복수
⑤ the horse - 3인칭 단수

01
'나'는 1인칭, '너'는 2인칭, '나'와 '너'를 뺀 나머지는 모두 3인칭 이다. 하나는 단수, 둘 이상은 복수이다.

02 다음 빈칸에 들어갈 말로 알맞은 것은 ?

_____ are very kind people.

① I
② Tom's nephew
③ He and she
④ She
⑤ He

02
people 사람들
nephew 조카

03 다음 빈칸에 들어갈 말로 알맞지 <u>않은</u> 것은?

_____ is a famous painter.

① My father
② Tom
③ She
④ Picasso
⑤ The men

03
famous 유명한
painter 화가
Picasso 피카소

04 다음 표현들 중에서 1인칭을 고르시오. (2개)

04

bicycle 자전거

your father	he	my bag	we	your feet
my face	I	the bicycles	she	you

05 다음 밑줄 친 부분 중 바르지 <u>않은</u> 것은?

I have a brother. He ① <u>is</u> ② <u>a</u> ③ <u>very</u> ④ <u>tall</u> ⑤ <u>boys</u>.

06 다음 문장 중 바른 것은?

① This is new hairpins.
② He is a scientist.
③ I am a lawyers.
④ It is a big boats.
⑤ Mary is my sisters.

06

scientist 과학자
lawyer 변호사

07 다음 중 단수형과 복수형이 잘못 짝지어진 것은?

① this – those
② I – we
③ you – you
④ he – they
⑤ she – they

08 다음 중 밑줄 친 부분의 쓰임이 다른 것은?

① <u>This</u> is Mr. Park.
② <u>This</u> is a watermelon.
③ <u>This</u> is my uncle.
④ <u>This</u> is my friend.
⑤ <u>This</u> is Korean.

08

watermelon 수박

this는 지시대명사로도
쓰이고 인칭대명사로도
쓰인다.

09 다음 빈칸에 들어갈 말로 알맞은 것은?

> Those are wonderful _____.

① coat
② watch
③ airplanes
④ dog
⑤ computer

10 다음 밑줄 친 You가 복수인 것은?

① <u>You</u> are a fire fighter.
② <u>You</u> are Bob's brother.
③ <u>You</u> are honest students.
④ <u>You</u> are Julia.
⑤ <u>You</u> are my cousin.

다음 주어진 단어를 알맞은 형태로 바꿔 빈칸에 써 보자.

1 _____ are engineers. (I)

2 _____ are sportsmen. (he)

3 _____ are a tall boy. (you)

4 They are good _____. (child)

5 _____ are kind women. (that)

6 She is my _____. (aunt)

7 _____ am a pianist. (I)

8 They are nice _____. (car)

9 _____ are good swimmers. (you)

10 This is an expensive _____. (house)

11 _____ are pretty roses. (this)

12 _____ are smart girls. (she)

13 We are good _____. (farmer)

14 _____ is a golfer. (he)

15 _____ are kind ladies. (you)

- **Review Test 1**
- **내신대비 1**

01 모음을 써 보자.

_____ , _____ , _____ , _____ , _____ ,

02 다음 중 보기에서 셀 수 있는 명사와 셀 수 없는 명사를 골라 써 보자.

1. coffee	2. pen	3. student	4. cheese	5. air
6. skirt	7. watch	8. bread	9. Coke	10. table

셀 수 있는 명사 _____ , _____ , _____ , _____ , _____ ,

셀 수 없는 명사 _____ , _____ , _____ , _____ , _____ ,

03 주어진 명사의 복수형을 골라 보자.

1   box   (boxs,   boxes)

2   knife   (knifes,   knives)

3   piano   (pianos,   pianoes)

4   deer   (deer,   deers)

5   candy   (candys,   candies)

6   watch   (watchs,   watches)

7   chair   (chaires,   chairs)

8   bus   (buses,   buss)

9   woman   (womans,   women)

10   foot   (feet,   foots)

04 다음 명사의 복수형을 써 보자.

1 dress

2 fish

3 city

4 room

5 church

6 potato

7 mouse

8 eraser

9 fox

10 tomato

11 fly

12 dish

13 zoo

14 child

15 tooth

01 다음 우리말에 맞도록 (   ) 안에서 알맞은 말을 골라 동그라미 해 보자.

1 콜라 2캔   two (cans, cartons) of Coke

2 한 가지 충고   a (piece, sheet) of advice

3 빵 5덩어리   five (loaves, bags) of bread

4 콜라 10잔   ten (glasses, cartons) of Coke

5 포도 7송이   seven (bowls, bunches) of grapes

6 피클 4병   four (loaves, jars) of pickles

7 차 6잔   six (cups, bars) of tea

8 쌀 2봉지   two (bags, bottles) of rice

9 치즈 5조각   five (sheets, slices) of cheese

10 우유 3팩   three (cups, cartons) of milk

11 종이2장   two (sheets, loaves) of (papers, paper)

12 가구 8점   eight (bars, pieces) of (furniture, furnitures)

13 옥수수 통조림 4캔   four (bottles, cans) of (corn, corns)

14 샴푸 7병   seven (cans, bottles) of shampoo

15 비누 3개   three (pieces, bars) of soap

O2 우리말에 맞도록 빈칸을 채워 보자.

1	바나나 3다발	three	of bananas
2	잼 2병	two	of jam
3	우유 3팩	three	of milk
4	설탕 4봉지	four	of sugar
5	콜라 5캔	five	of Coke
6	물 3병	three	of water
7	두 가지 충고	two	of advice
8	우유 6잔	six	of milk
9	초콜릿 5개	five	of chocolate
10	음악 1곡	a	of music
11	치약 10개	ten	of toothpaste
12	바나나 8다발	eight	of bananas
13	주스 5병	five	of juice
14	담요 4장	four	of blanket
15	정보 한 가지	a	of information

01   다음 ( ) 안에서 알맞은 말을 골라 동그라미 해 보자.

1 Mary is (a, an, the, ×) my sister.

2 This is my mom's bag. (A, An, The, ×) bag is cheap.

3 It is (a, an, the, ×) old clock.

4 They are (a, an, the, ×) lawyers.

5 He has (a, an, the, ×) dinner at six.

6 We live on (a, an, the, ×) earth.

7 There is (a, an, the, ×) Yonsei university in Shinchon.

8 (A, An, The, ×) book is on the table. (A, An, The, ×) book is mine.

9 She plays (a, an, the, ×) cello.

10 Tom goes to (a, an, the, ×) East sea.

11 My friends enjoy playing (a, an, the, ×) basketball.

12 He has (a, an, the, ×) elephant.

13 James wants to be (a, an, the, ×) fire fighter.

14 The coffee is (a, an, the, ×) hot.

15 Tom's family stays in (a, an, the, ×) Grand hotel.

02 다음 빈칸에 a, an, the를 쓰거나, 필요 없는 곳에 ×표를 해 보자.

1 Mary is _____ very nice dancer.

2 _____ sun rises in _____ east.

3 She speaks _____ English well.

4 This is _____ his tie.

5 I have _____ dog. Its name is 'Odda'

6 She buys _____ shirt. _____ shirt is too big for me.

7 He arrives at _____ Kennedy airport.

8 Do you have his _____ pen?

9 He jumps up in _____ air.

10 They have _____ dinner at 8.

11 His brothers play _____ flute.

12 We look around _____ Louvre museum. Louvre museum 루브르 박물관

13 The boys get some apples. _____ apples are sweet.

14 Tom eats lunch at _____ Burger King's.

15 There is a korean restaurant on _____ Main Street.

01 다음 중 모음끼리 이루어진 것은?

① reu
② apo
③ eiu
④ oec
⑤ aif

02 다음에서 모음을 찾아 ○표 해 보세요.

> Wow! It's a beautiful mountain.

03 다음 중 셀 수 <u>없는</u> 명사 2개는?

① egg
② cat
③ milk
④ juice
⑤ boy

04 다음 중 단수형과 복수형이 바르게 짝지어 진 것은?

① baby - babys
② bed - beds
③ dish -dishies
④ ball- balles
⑤ leaf -leafs

05 주어진 명사들의 복수형을 만들 때, 공통으로 뒤에 붙는 것은?

> dish　glass　box　church
> potato

① s
② es
③ ves
④ ies
⑤ ss

06 단수형을 복수형으로 고친 것입니다. 바르게 고쳐 보세요.

> knife → knifes

_____ ⇨ _____

O7 다음 중 단수형과 복수형이 잘못 짝지어진 것은?

① candy - candys
② watch - watches
③ eye -eyes
④ knife -knives
⑤ fox - foxes

O8 명사의 복수형입니다. 밑줄친 곳에 들어갈 알맞은 것은?

fly – fl_____
house – house_____

① s - es
② es - ies
③ es - s
④ ies - s
⑤ s - s

O9 다음 중 an을 붙일 수 있는 것 둘을 고르면?

① book
② egg
③ orange
④ dog
⑤ hat

10 다음 중 a나 an이 들어갈 수 있는 곳은 모두 골라 보세요.

① I want _____ pen.
② He eats _____ apple.
③ Ann goes to _____ America.
④ They eat _____ milk.
⑤ Mom meets _____ Jane.

11 다음 중 어법상 옳지 않은 것을 골라 보세요.

① She plays the piano.
② Tom has the lunch.
③ He plays tennis.
④ We eat dinner.
⑤ They play basketball.

12 다음 중 **틀린** 곳을 바르게 고쳐 보세요.

> Bill gets up at 7.
> He eats the breakfast at 7:30.
> He goes to school at 8.

_____ ⇨ _____

13 밑줄 친 곳에 들어갈 것은?

> I have _____ cat.
> _____ cat is white.

① a - An
② an - A
③ the - A
④ the - An
⑤ a - The

14 다음 중 밑줄 친 곳에 공통으로 들어갈 수 있는 것은?

> _____ butter, _____ bag

① a
② an
③ the

15 다음 중 밑줄 친 곳에 the가 들어갈 수 있는 것은?

① He plays _____ soccer.
② I play _____ cello.
③ She has _____ breakfast.
④ They have _____ supper.
⑤ Dad plays _____ golf.

정답 및 해설 p.9

16 다음 중 어법상 옳은 것은?

① A rose is in the vase.
② I know a Ann.
③ I eat a bread.
④ She leaves for a China.
⑤ He gives me a books.

17 틀린 곳을 올바르게 고친 것은?

Jane plays violin everyday.

① Jane plays a violins everyday.
② Jane plays a violin everyday.
③ Jane plays an violin everyday.
④ Jane plays the violins everyday.
⑤ Jane plays the violin everyday.

18 빈칸에 알맞은 관사를 써 보세요.

I read a book. _____ book is fun.

19 밑줄 친 곳에 들어갈 수 <u>없는</u> 것은?

_____ are nice guys.

① We
② You
③ These
④ Those
⑤ He

20 다음 중 옳은 문장 두 개를 고르면?

① I am a doctors.
② You are doctors.
③ He is doctors.
④ Jane is a doctors.
⑤ We are doctors.

21 다음 중 밑줄 친 곳에 the가 들어갈 수 있는 것을 모두 골라 보자.

① He has _____ lunch.
② I pick an apple. _____ apple is red.
③ We play _____ football.
④ My mom plays _____ golf.
⑤ My sister plays _____ piano.

22 다음 중 옳지 <u>않은</u> 것은?

① watches - 시계들
② hens - 암탉들
③ couches - 긴 의자들
④ babys - 아기들
⑤ monkeys - 원숭이들

23 주어진 명사를 복수형으로 바꿔 써 보자.

a. room   –

b. wolf   –

c. fox   –

24 a나 an 중에 하나를 골라 순서대로 써 보자.

I buy _____ eraser.

He eats _____ cookie.

–

25 셀 수 <u>없는</u> 명사로 묶은 것은?

① house, butter, pencil
② money, student, goose
③ water, bread, pillow
④ honey, shoes, glass
⑤ juice, money, sugar

pillow 베개

Unit o5

지시대명사와 지시형용사

지시대명사는 사물을 가리키는 대명사,
지시형용사는 뒤에 있는 명사를 꾸며주는
형용사 역할을 한다.

지시대명사와 지시형용사

지시대명사는 우리 말로 '이것(들), 저것(들)'로 해석되지만, 지시형용사는 뒤에 나온 명사를 꾸며주므로 '이~, 저~'로 해석된다.

 1 지시대명사와 지시형용사의 차이점

지시대명사	지시형용사
사물을 가리키는 대명사	사물을 가리키는 형용사로 바로 뒤에 명사가 온다.
this, that these, those	this cap, that cap these caps, those caps

ex. **This** is my book.   이것은 나의 책이다.
지시대명사

This book is mine.   이 책은 나의 것이다.
지시형용사 명사

These are your pens.   이것들은 너의 펜(들)이다.
지시대명사

These pens are yours.   이 펜들은 너의 것이다.
지시형용사   명사

cf. **It** is his cap.   그것은 그의 모자이다.

The cap is his.   그 모자는 그의 것이다.

The caps are his.   그 모자들은 그의 것이다.

 형용사란?
명사를 꾸며주는 역할을 하는 말이다.   *ex.* He is a good boy.   그는 착한 소년이다.
형용사 명사

Tip! The cap의 The는 지시형용사가 아니고 정관사이지만 this book(이 책), that book(저 책)에 이어 the book(그 책)을 연속적으로 알아두어야 할 필요가 있다. 아울러, that은 우리말의 '그, 저'로 대응되어 사용하기도 한다는 것을 기억해 두자.

「지시형용사 + 명사」의 수의 일치

지시형용사 this, that 다음에는 반드시 단수명사가 오고, these, those 다음에는 반드시 복수명사가 온다.

this, that + 단수명사	this flower, that flower
these, those + 복수명사	**these** flowers, **those** flowers

> **Tip!** 지시형용사 this, that 다음에는 단수명사가 오고, these, those 다음에는 복수 명사가 오지만, 정관사 the 뒤에는 단수명사와 복수명사 둘 다 올 수 있다.
> *ex.* the cat (o)   the cats (o)

① 대명사로 받기

▶ 보통 앞에 나온 명사가 뒤에 다시 언급될 때 대명사로 받아 준다.

ex. Mary is pretty.

Tom is handsome.

The boys are my students.

The bag is old.

She is my daughter.   그녀는 나의 딸이다.

He is your friend.   그는 너의 친구이다.

They are very tall.   그들은 매우 크다.

It is Bill's.   그것은 Bill의 것이다.

▶ 앞에 나온 '대명사와 대명사', '명사와 대명사', '명사와 명사'를 다시 언급할 때 대명사로 받는다.

1인칭인 I와 함께 있으면	we로 받는다.
2인칭인 you와 함께 있으면	you로 받는다.
3인칭끼리 있으면	they로 받는다.

ex. Jane and I are doctors.

Tom and **you** study hard.

Jane and he are good swimmers.

A dog and a cat are under the table.

So **we** are busy.   그래서 우리는 바쁘다.

So **you** are always tired.
그래서 너희들은 항상 피곤하다.

They are famous.   그들은 유명하다.

They are friends.   그들은 친구이다.

> **Tip!** my father나 your father처럼 명사 앞에 소유격이 오면 I나 you로 받는 것으로 착각하기도 한다.
> my father는 나의 아버지이지 '나'는 아니므로 3인칭 단수 he로 받아야 한다.

밑줄 친 부분이 지시대명사인지 지시형용사인지 동그라미 해 보자.

garden 정원
necklace 목걸이
sweet potato 고구마

* this(these), that(those)
는 바로 뒤에 명사가 오면
명사를 꾸며 주는 지시
형용사가 된다.

1 <u>This</u> is a book.   (지시대명사, 지시형용사)

2 <u>Those</u> horses are Miss Park's.   (지시대명사, 지시형용사)

3 <u>That</u> flower is a lily.   (지시대명사, 지시형용사)

4 <u>It</u> is his pizza.   (지시대명사, 지시형용사)

5 <u>These</u> houses are white.   (지시대명사, 지시형용사)

6 <u>That</u> is my dress.   (지시대명사, 지시형용사)

7 <u>They</u> are onions.   (지시대명사, 지시형용사)

8 <u>Those</u> are tomatoes.   (지시대명사, 지시형용사)

9 <u>This</u> ruler is very long.   (지시대명사, 지시형용사)

10 <u>That</u> is Mr. Kang.   (지시대명사, 지시형용사)

11 <u>It</u> is a beautiful garden.   (지시대명사, 지시형용사)

12 <u>These</u> necklaces are expensive.   (지시대명사, 지시형용사)

13 <u>They</u> are snakes.   (지시대명사, 지시형용사)

14 <u>This</u> sweet potato is very sweet.   (지시대명사, 지시형용사)

15 <u>Those</u> students are hungry.   (지시대명사, 지시형용사)

2

알맞은 말을 골라 동그라미 해 보자.

1 these (dog, (dogs))
this (dog, dogs)
this (rice, rices)

2 those (picture, pictures)
that (picture, pictures)
that (chocolate, chocolates)

3 the (dresses, dress) 그 드레스
the (dresses, dress) 그 드레스들
the (Coke, Cokes)

picture 그림
cell phone 휴대폰

알맞은 말을 골라 동그라미 해 보자.

1 (that, those) pen
(that, those) pens
(that, those) money

2 (this, these) cell phones
(this, these) cell phone
(this, these) paper

3 the (soap, soaps)
the (pot, pots) 그 냄비들
the (pot, pots) 그 냄비

다음을 알맞은 대명사로 바꾼 것을 골라 동그라미 해 보자.

kitten 새끼고양이
daughter 딸
crocodile 악어

1 my sister and she   ((they), we)

2 he and I   (they, we)

3 Misun and you   (we, you)

4 my mother   (he, she)

5 his friend and you   (they, you)

6 Jimmy, Paul and I   (you, we)

7 the kitten   (he, it)

8 the teacher and his daughter   (they, she)

9 he and she   (you, they)

10 Mary, Giho and you   (you, they)

11 a crocodile   (it, he)

12 Jane and Paul   (she, they)

13 your uncles   (they, he)

14 your uncle   (she, he)

15 the airplanes   (it, they)

4

다음을 알맞은 대명사로 바꿔 써 보자.

1 the bus   *it*

2 Jinsu and I

3 her boyfriend

4 a woman

5 an apple and two pears

6 the umbrellas

7 Suho, Insuk and Paul

8 he and you

9 Jim and I

10 a man

11 your cats

12 the rose

13 a classroom

14 he, she and you

15 the foxes

pear 배
umbrella 우산
classroom 교실

다음을 복수형으로 옳게 바꾼 것을 골라 ○표 해 보자.

vest 조끼
barber 이발사
lily 백합

1 that bus   (those bus, (those buses))

2 this boy   (these boy, these boys)

3 that sheep   (those sheeps, those sheep)

4 that sweater   (that sweaters, those sweaters)

5 the vest   (the vests, these vests)

6 this letter   (these letter, these letters)

7 that train   (that trains, those trains)

8 this pencil   (these pencil, these pencils)

9 that barber   (that barbers, those barbers)

10 the sofa   (they sofas, the sofas)

11 that fish   (those fish, that fish)

12 that man   (that men, those men)

13 this lily   (these lilies, this lilies)

14 the tooth   (the teeth, the toothes)

15 this leaf   (those leaves, these leaves)

2

다음을 복수형으로 옳게 바꾼 것을 골라 ○표 해 보자.

1 that ring   (those rings, that rings)

2 this ox   (these oxen, this oxen)

3 the man   (the mans, the men)

4 the baby   (the babies, they babies)

5 that mouse   (that mice, those mice)

6 the photo   (the photoes, the photos)

7 this video   (these videos, this videos)

8 that carrot   (those carrot, those carrots)

9 that chief   (those chieves, those chiefs)

10 the elephant   (the elephants, these elephants)

11 this lady   (this ladies, these ladies)

12 that kid   (that kids, those kids)

13 that ship   (those ships, those ship)

14 this jumper   (this jumpers, these jumpers)

15 the woman   (the women, they women)

carrot 당근
chief 의장
elephant 코끼리
ship 배

다음을 복수형으로 바꿔 써 보자.

ant 개미
snake 뱀
bug 벌레
deer 사슴

1 that ant   *those ants*

2 this zoo

3 the bench

4 that snake

5 this bug

6 the hot dog

7 this memo

8 that mouse

9 that foot

10 this piano

11 that city

12 this truck

13 the glass

14 that sportsman

15 this deer

4

다음을 복수형으로 바꿔 써 보자.

1 that city   *those cities*

2 the model

3 this taxi

4 this cello

5 the child

6 that dish

7 that melon

8 the flower

9 that sweet potato

10 this train

11 that farmer

12 this knife

13 the baby

14 that violin

15 the cookie

city 도시
model 모델
dish 접시
farmer 농부

주어진 우리말을 영어로 옮겨 보자.

pot 냄비
computer 컴퓨터
glove 장갑
church 교회
paper 종이

1 이 책들   *these books*

2 저 책상

3 그 냄비들

4 그 주스

5 저 황소들

6 이 코트

7 이 컴퓨터들

8 저 장난감들

9 그 장갑들

10 이 학생

11 저 빵

12 그 인형

13 이 사탕들

14 그 교회들

15 이 종이

6

주어진 우리말을 영어로 옮겨 보자.

1 이 물   *this water*

2 그 보트들

3 저 가게

4 그 토마토들

5 저 호랑이들

6 이 사진

7 그 스카프들

8 저 치즈

9 이 기름

10 그 요리사

11 저 선풍기

12 그 버터

13 저 양말들

14 이 의사들

15 저 버스들

boat 보트
store 가게
picture 사진
fan 선풍기
butter 버터
socks 양말

다음 단수형을 복수형으로 바꾼 것이다. **틀린** 곳에 밑줄을 치고 바르게 고쳐 써 보자.

strawberry 딸기

	단수형	복수형	
1	that star	→ those <u>star</u>	*stars*
2	the desk	→ they desks	
3	this chef	→ this chefs	
4	this tulip	→ these tulip	
5	that computer	→ that computers	
6	this deer	→ these deers	
7	the video	→ the videoes	
8	that strawberry	→ those strawberry	
9	this map	→ these map	
10	this baby	→ this babies	
11	this sheep	→ these sheeps	
12	the leaf	→ they leaves	
13	that lamp	→ those lamp	
14	this ring	→ this rings	
15	that postman	→ those postman	

2

다음 명사를 대명사로 받은 것이다. 바르게 고쳐 써 보자.

1	your aunts	→ she	*they*
2	Sumi and I	→ they	
3	his niece	→ he	
4	Joe, Rex and you	→ we	
5	a sunflower	→ they	
6	your grandson	→ she	
7	he and she	→ we	
8	the students	→ he	
9	Insuk, Judy and I	→ you	
10	she and her friend	→ we	
11	an actress	→ he	
12	your nephew	→ she	
13	the albums	→ you	
14	my grandparents	→ we	
15	Joe and you	→ we	

niece 여자 조카
sunflower 해바라기
grandson 손자
actress 여자 배우
nephew 남자 조카
grandparents 조부모님

6 your 너의

10 her 그녀의

01 다음 중 밑줄 친 <u>This</u>의 쓰임이 <u>다른</u> 것은?

① <u>This</u> is a wet towel.
② <u>This</u> is a wonderful picture.
③ <u>This</u> cellphone is very expensive.
④ <u>This</u> is a very nice train.
⑤ <u>This</u> is a big vase.

01

wet 젖은

this(these),
that(those) 뒤에
명사가 와서 그 명사를
꾸며 주면 이를 지시
형용사라고 한다.

02 다음 중 대명사로 바꾼 것 중 올바른 것은?

① your mouth → you
② Mr. Han and Mrs. Han → we
③ John and you → they
④ my brothers → he
⑤ Joe and I → we

03 다음 중 대명사로 바꾼 것 중 <u>잘못된</u> 것은?

① she and I → they
② my sister → she
③ the man → he
④ Jane's friends → they
⑤ he and I → we

04 다음 단수형을 복수형으로 바꾼 것 중 바르지 <u>않은</u> 것은?

① this cap → these caps
② that notebook → those notebooks
③ the deer → the deer
④ this watch → these watches
⑤ that memo → that memos

04

복수형으로 고칠 때는 지시형용사와 명사 모두를 복수형으로 바꿔 주어야 한다.

정답 및 해설 p.11

05 다음 빈칸에 들어갈 말이 순서대로 바르게 짝지어진 것은?

> Tommy, Joe and you are good students.
>
> = _____ are good _____.

① They – students
② Those – students
③ You – student
④ We – student
⑤ You – students

[06-07] 다음 빈칸에 들어갈 말이 순서대로 바르게 짝지어진 것을 고르시오.

06
- _____ cartoons are so funny.
- _____ coins are gold.

① Those - They
② That - These
③ They - These
④ Those - These
⑤ Those - This

06

cartoon 만화
funny 재미있는,
우스꽝스러운

07
- _____ chairs are old.
- _____ fox is hungry.

① This - These
② These - Those
③ That - Those
④ This - That
⑤ These - That

[08-09] 다음 문장을 단수형으로 바꿀 때, 빈칸에 알맞은 말을 쓰시오.

더 알아보기

08

The cucumbers are very fresh.

→ _____ _____ is very fresh.

08

the는 지시형용사가 아니라 정관사이므로, 뒤에 단수형과 복수형 명사 둘 다 올 수 있다.

09

Those school bags are mine.

→ _____ _____ is mine.

09

mine 나의 것

10 다음 빈칸에 알맞은 대명사를 쓰시오.

Mr. Kim and Mrs. Kim are very great artists.

= _____ are very great artists.

10

great 훌륭한, 위대한

다음을 대명사로 바꿔 보자.

1 my nose

2 the girl

3 our house

4 her son and you

5 his sister and I

6 cars

7 a violin

8 Tom, Ann and my sister

다음 주어진 단어를 알맞은 형태로 바꿔 빈칸 안에 써 보자.

1 These   are very wild. (wolf)

2 That   is black. (box)

3 The   is my sister. (nurse)

4 This   is good. (soap)

5 These   are red. (roof)

6 Those   are fresh. (orange)

7 Look at   zebras! (that)

8 The   are my cousins. (girl)   cousin 사촌

Unit **06**

인칭대명사의
격변화

영어의 인칭대명사는
격에 따라 형태가 달라진다.
즉, 주격, 소유격, 목적격,
소유대명사의 형태가 각기 다르다.

Unit 06 인칭대명사의 격변화

1 인칭대명사의 격변화

우리말에서는 인칭대명사의 주격, 소유격, 목적격, 소유대명사를 나타낼 때, 조사를 써서 다음과 같이 나타낸다.

인칭대명사
(나, 너, 그, 그녀, 우리, 너희들, 그들…) +

~은, ~는, ~이, ~가	(주격)
~의	(소유격)
~을, ~를, ~에게	(목적격)
~의 것	(소유대명사)

하지만, 영어에서는 인칭대명사의 격에 따라 각기 다른 형태의 단어를 사용하므로, 반드시 외워 두자.

▶ 「나는 그를 사랑한다.」를 영어로 써 보자.

ex. I love <u>he</u>.   나는 **그는** 사랑한다.
           그는

   I love <u>his</u>.   나는 **그의** 사랑한다.
           그의

   I love <u>him</u>.   나는 **그를** 사랑한다.
           그를

▶ 「이것은 나의 책이다.」를 영어로 표현해 보자.

ex. This is <u>I</u> book.   이것은 **나는** 책이다.
            나는

   This is <u>me</u> book.   이것은 **나를** 책이다.
            나를

   This is <u>my</u> book.   이것은 **나의** 책이다.
            나의

이와 같이 격에 알맞은 인칭대명사를 사용하여야 한다.

인칭대명사/의문사 who의 격변화와 소유대명사

열 번씩 큰소리로 읽어 보자. ○○○○○ ○○○○○

종류		주격	소유격	목적격	소유대명사
단수	1인칭	I 나는	my 나의	me 나를(에게)	mine 나의 것
	2인칭	you 너는	your 너의	you 너를(에게)	yours 너의 것
	3인칭	he 그는	his 그의	him 그를(에게)	his 그의 것
		she 그녀는	her 그녀의	her 그녀를(에게)	hers 그녀의 것
		it 그것은	its 그것의	it 그것을(에게)	–
복수	1인칭	we 우리들은	our 우리들의	us 우리들을(에게)	ours 우리들의 것
	2인칭	you 너희들은	your 너희들의	you 너희들을(에게)	yours 너희들의 것
	3인칭	they 그(것)들은	their 그(것)들의	them 그(것)들을(에게)	theirs 그(것)들의 것
의문사 who		who 누가	whose 누구의	whom 누구를(에게)	whose 누구의 것

* 의문사는 3권에서 자세히 배우기로 한다.

 명사의 격변화와 소유대명사

종류	주격	소유격	목적격	소유대명사
고유명사	Tom Tom은	Tom's Tom의	Tom Tom을(에게)	Tom's Tom의 것
보통 명사	my sister 나의 여동생은	my sister's 나의 여동생의	my sister 나의 여동생을(에게)	my sister's 나의 여동생의 것

빈칸을 채워 인칭대명사와 who의 격변화와 소유대명사를 완성해 보자.

종류		주격	소유격	목적격	소유대명사
단수	1인칭	I 나는	나의	나를(에게)	mine 나의 것
	2인칭	you 너는	your 너의	you 너를(에게)	너의 것
	3인칭	그는	그의	him 그를(에게)	그의 것
		she	her	그녀를(에게)	그녀의 것
		it 그것은	그것의	그것을(에게)	− −
복수	1인칭	우리들은	our	우리들을(에게)	우리들의 것
	2인칭	you	너희들의	you	너희들의 것
	3인칭	they 그(것)들은	그(것)들의	그(것)들을(에게)	theirs
의문사 who		who	누구의	누구를(에게)	whose

빈칸을 채워 명사의 격변화와 소유대명사를 완성해 보자.

종류	주격	소유격	목적격	소유대명사
고유명사	Tom Tom은	Tom의	Tom	Tom의 것
보통명사	my sister 나의 여동생은	나의 여동생의	나의 여동생을(에게)	my sister's

2

다음 ( ) 안에서 알맞은 우리말을 골라 동그라미 해 보자. (2가지 가능)

1 I 나(는, 를/에게)

2 his 그(를/에게, 의 것)

3 them 그들(의, 을/에게)

4 ours 우리들(을/에게, 의 것)

5 you 너(의, 를/에게)

6 my sister's 나의 여동생(의, 를)

7 our 우리들(의, 의 것)

8 whose 누구(의, 을/에게)

9 Tom Tom(을/에게, 의 것)

10 us 우리들(의, 을/에게)

11 she 그녀(는, 의 것)

12 Tom's Tom(을/에게, 의)

13 it 그것(의, 을/에게)

14 him 그(는, 를/에게)

15 they 그들(은, 을/에게)

16 her 그녀(를/에게, 의 것)

17 mine 나(를/에게, 의 것)

18 whom 누구(의, 를/에게)

19 we 우리들(은, 의 것)

20 my 나(의, 의 것)

21 whose 누구(를/에게, 의 것)

22 you 너(를/에게, 의 것)

23 theirs 그들(의, 의 것)

24 their 그들(의, 의 것)

25 my sister 나의 여동생(은, 의)

26 he 그(는, 을/에게)

27 you 너희들(은, 의 것)

28 hers 그녀(를/에게, 의 것)

29 Tom's Tom(을/에게, 의 것)

30 it 그것(은, 의 것)

9 고유 명사의 목적격은
형태의 변화 없이 그대로
사용한다.

다음 ( ) 안에서 알맞은 인칭대명사를 골라 동그라미 해 보자.

1 나를 ((me), mine)　　　　**2** 그의 것 (his, him)

3 그를(에게) (his, him)　　　　**4** 그것들을(에게) (their, them)

5 너를(에게) (your, you)　　　　**6** 나의 여동생의 것
　　　　　　　　　　　　　　(my sister, my sister's)

7 우리들의 (our, ours)　　　　**8** 누구의 (whose, whom)

9 Tom을(에게) (Tom, Tom's)　　**10** 우리들을(에게) (our, us)

11 그녀의 (her, hers)　　　　**12** Tom의 (Tom, Tom's)

13 그것은 (it, its)　　　　**14** 그의 (his, him)

15 그들을(에게) (they, them)　　**16** 그녀를(에게) (her, hers)

17 나의 것 (my, mine)　　　　**18** 그들의 (their, them)

19 우리들은 (we, us)　　　　**20** 나의 (my, mine)

21 누구를(에게) (whose, whom)　**22** 너는 (you, your)

23 그들의 것 (them, theirs)　　**24** 그것들의 (their, them)

25 나의 여동생을(에게)　　　　**26** 그는 (he, him)
　　(my sister's, my sister)

27 너희들을(에게) (you, your)　**28** 그녀의 것 (her, hers)

29 Tom의 것 (Tom, Tom's)　　**30** 그것을(에게) (it, its)

4

다음 빈칸에 알맞은 인칭대명사를 써 보자.

1 그녀의 　　　her	2 Tom의 것
3 나를(에게)	4 누가
5 그들의 것	6 너의 것
7 너를(에게)	8 그를(에게)
9 그것을(에게)	10 나의 여동생을(에게)
11 너희들의 것	12 누구를(에게)
13 우리들은	14 그녀는
15 그의 것	16 Tom의
17 너의	18 그것들을(에게)
19 Tom을(에게)	20 우리들의 것
21 누구의	22 그것의
23 나의 것	24 우리들을(에게)
25 너희들의	26 나의 여동생의
27 그것들의	28 누구의 것
29 나의	30 그들의

다음 빈칸에 알맞은 인칭대명사를 써 보자.

1	너의	*your*	
2	누구의 것		
3	그것들을		
4	그의		
5	그들은		
6	그것들의		
7	그녀를(에게)		
8	나를(에게)		
9	나의		
10	그녀의 것		
11	누구를(에게)		
12	그들을(에게)		
13	그녀의		
14	Tom은		
15	그를(에게)		
16	우리들의 것		
17	나의 여동생의 것		
18	그녀를(에게)		
19	나의 것		
20	Tom의		
21	우리들을(에게)		
22	누구의		
23	그것의		
24	우리들의		
25	그의 것		
26	너희들을(에게)		
27	그들의		
28	너의 것		
29	너는		
30	나의 여동생의		

6

다음 빈칸에 알맞은 인칭대명사를 써 보자.

1 누구의	*whose*	**2** 너를	
3 그들의		**4** 그녀의 것	
5 우리들을		**6** 그것의	
7 그의		**8** Tom을	
9 나의 것		**10** 누구의 것	
11 그들을		**12** 너희들의 것	
13 너희들의		**14** 나의 여동생을	
15 Tom의 것		**16** 그는	
17 그녀의		**18** 너의	
19 우리는		**20** 누구를	
21 그의 것		**22** 나의 여동생의 것	
23 그녀를		**24** 그들의 것	
25 우리의 것		**26** 너희들을	
27 너의 것		**28** Tom의	
29 우리의		**30** 그를	

다음 (   ) 안에서 알맞은 말을 골라 동그라미 해 보자.

chicken 닭
write 쓰다
invite 초대하다
hug 안아주다
bat 막대기, 방망이
album 앨범
on Sundays 일요일마다

1 They are (my, mine, me) cats.

2 Those watches are (Judy, Judy's).

3 (It, Its) is my lemon.

4 That is (the boy, the boy's) bicycle.

5 The chickens are (he, him, his).

6 (We, Our, Us, Ours) write some letters.

7 Jimmy invites (they, their, them, theirs).

8 My father hugs (I, my, me, mine).

9 These bats are (they, their, them, theirs).

10 The dog is (you, your, yours).

11 Tom likes (she, her).

12 These albums are (she, her, hers).

13 That is (we, our, us, ours) school.

14 (You, Your, Yours) love (it, its).

15 (Her, Hers, She) goes to church on Sundays.

8

다음 (   ) 안에서 알맞은 말을 골라 동그라미 해 보자.

1 Those are ((their), they, them, theirs) cups.

2 She likes to swim with (I, my, me).

3 (Tom, Tom's) reads a newspaper.

4 Those horses are (we, our, us, ours).

5 This pear is (she, her, hers).

6 (They, Their, Them, Theirs) are (he, his, him) radishes.

7 Those are (we, our, us, ours) stick candies.

8 (She, Her, Hers) eyes are small.

9 (You, Your, Yours) are (I, my, me, mine) best friend.

10 Those erasers are (I, my, me, mine).

11 (She, Her, Hers) knows (we, our, us).

12 The elephants are (they, their, them, theirs).

13 Tom brushes (he, his, him) teeth.

14 Those are (you, your, yours) shorts.

15 (My sister, My sister's) house is next to the hospital.

---

newspaper 신문
pear (먹는)배
radish 무
stick candy 막대사탕
know 알다
shorts 반바지
next to~ ~ 옆에
hospital 병원

2 with, for, of, to…
등의 전치사 뒤에는
목적격 대명사가 온다.

다음 (　) 안에서 알맞은 말을 골라 동그라미 해 보자.

vest 조끼
give 주다
buy 사다, 사 주다
miss 그리워하다
racket 라켓
peach 복숭아
bring 가져오다, 가져다 주다
digital camera 디지털
카메라
teach 가르치다

1 (We, Our, Us, Ours) run fast.

2 This is (you, your, yours) vest.

3 Mary gives (he, his, him) a piece of cake.

4 He buys (we, our, us) a book.

5 I miss (you, your, yours).

6 (They, Their, Them) rackets are new.

7 The pink pants are (Jane's, Jane).

8 Those peaches are (you, your, yours).

9 This is for (he, his, him).

10 The building is (my father, my father's).

11 That is (she, her, hers) digital camera.

12 Tom and (I, me) go shopping with (her, hers).

13 I bring (she, her, hers) a chair.

14 These fish are (we, our, us, ours).

15 You teach (the boy, the boy's) English.

2

다음 (   ) 안에서 알맞은 말을 골라 동그라미 해 보자.

1 Mom wakes (my, me, mine) up early in the morning.

2 (Mr. Kim, Mr. Kim's) is (he, his, him) uncle.

3 She talks to (we, our, us, ours).

4 These clothes are (they, their, them, theirs).

5 (She, Her, Hers) sits next to (he, his, him).

6 The scarf is (she, her, hers).

7 They visit (we, our, us, ours).

8 (He, His, Him) helps (I, my, me, mine).

9 He takes care of (they, their, them, theirs).

10 This man is (she, her, hers) father.

11 Mom gives (Jane, Jane's) some apples.

12 (It, Its) color is brown.

13 (He, His, Him) sister is young.

14 Those pineapples are (she, her, hers).

15 (She, Her, Hers) sends her thanks to (you, your, yours).

wake 깨우다
early 일찍
talk 말하다
clothes 옷
scarf 스카프
take care of ~을 돌보다
give 주다
pineapple 파인애플
send 보내다
thank 감사

다음 빈칸에 ( ) 안의 대명사와 명사를 알맞은 형태로 고쳐 써 보자.

call 전화하다
sell 팔다
roller blade 롤러블레이드
look over 훑어보다
report 보고서
boil 끓이다
duck 오리
make 만들다, 만들어 주다
dirty 더러운
desktop computer
탁상용 컴퓨터
boots 장화, 부츠

1 He calls _my_ grandfather. (I)

2 _____ sells many roller blades. (she)

3 These maps are _____. (they)

4 She chats with _____. (he)

5 He looks over _____ report. (she)

6 She boils _____. (it)

7 It is _____ duck. (you)

8 Paul makes _____ a desk. (she)

9 The concert tickets are _____. (we)

10 Mr. Brown speaks in English to _____. (Ann)

11 These dirty shirts are _____. (he)

12 Those are _____ desktop computers. (they)

13 This chocolate is _____. (she)

14 They are _____ boots. (I)

15 I know _____. (he)

4

다음 빈칸에 ( ) 안의 대명사와 명사를 알맞은 형태로 고쳐 써 보자.

1　She forgets _the man's_ name. (the man)

2　They go to church with ＿＿＿＿＿. (we)

3　He eats ＿＿＿＿＿ hamburger. (Sumi)

4　＿＿＿＿＿ nose is long. (it)

5　She goes to the river with ＿＿＿＿＿. (they)

6　We are ＿＿＿＿＿ grandparents. (she)

7　Those apples are ＿＿＿＿＿. (Sujin)

8　Paul hides ＿＿＿＿＿. (she)

9　This cell phone is ＿＿＿＿＿. (I)

10　＿＿＿＿＿ remember ＿＿＿＿＿. (they, she)

11　＿＿＿＿＿ bird is smart. (he)

12　God loves ＿＿＿＿＿. (we)

13　These onions are ＿＿＿＿＿. (the farmer)

14　Mr. Park is ＿＿＿＿＿ boss. (I)

15　Those lilies are ＿＿＿＿＿. (we)

forget 잊다
river 강
grandparents 조부모님
hide 숨기다
God 신
onion 양파
boss 상사, 사장
lily 백합

다음 빈칸에 (   ) 안의 대명사와 명사를 알맞은 형태로 고쳐 써 보자.

cheap 값싼
ill 아픈
look 보이다
schoolbag 책가방
hard 열심히
in front of ~의 앞에
strawberry 딸기
jacket 쟈켓
kite 연

1 He skates with _us_ . (we)

2 _____ hairpin is very cheap. (she)

3 _____ looks very ill. (he)

4 I kiss _____ . (he)

5 Those schoolbags are _____ . (we)

6 _____ parents are American. (the boy)

7 We study hard with _____ . (James)

8 I am in front of _____ . (he)

9 _____ father has a big truck. (she)

10 These strawberries are _____ . (he)

11 _____ shirts are blue. (we)

12 He takes _____ jacket. (Insu)

13 That kite is _____ . (I)

14 _____ run to school every day. (you)

15 _____ is kind to _____ . (she, you)

6

다음 빈칸에 (   ) 안의 대명사와 명사를 알맞은 형태로 고쳐 써 보자.

1 I chase _them_ . (they)

2 _____ mom cooks in the kitchen. (I)

3 We believe _____ . (she)

4 That sweet potato is _____ . (Mary)

5 These socks are _____ . (you)

6 You show _____ the way. (I)

7 She is _____ niece. (we)

8 You wait for _____ . (they)

9 This is _____ comb. (Jane)

10 She always looks for _____ in the library. (we)

11 Those textbooks are _____ . (they)

12 _____ hat is yellow. (you)

13 She breaks _____ . (it)

14 _____ takes a walk. (he)

15 _____ puppies are lazy. (they)

chase 뒤쫓다
cook 요리하다
believe 믿다
show 보여주다
wait for ~을 기다리다
comb 빗
look for ~을 찾다
library 도서관
textbook 교과서
break 부수다
take a walk 산책하다
puppy 강아지
lazy 게으른

다음 밑줄 친 부분들 중에서 <u>틀린</u> 곳을 바르게 고쳐 써 보자.

take care of ~을 돌보다
voice 목소리
coin 동전
middle school 중학교

1 Jane is <u>him</u> <u>girl friend</u>.
              his

2 These donuts are <u>my</u>.

3 He <u>remembers</u> <u>she</u>.

4 <u>She</u> meets <u>their</u>.

5 My mom takes care of <u>we</u> <u>with</u> love.

6 <u>We</u> <u>pictures</u> are wonderful.

7 <u>Mr. Park</u> brings <u>I</u> coat.

8 <u>I</u> hear <u>hers</u> voice.

9 These are <u>mine</u> <u>coins</u>.

10 <u>This</u> is <u>they</u> gold.

11 <u>My</u> have too much <u>money</u>.

12 <u>Jennys</u> <u>keys</u> are in her car.

13 The red <u>tomatoes</u> are <u>the farmer</u>.

14 I buy <u>his</u> a <u>guitar</u>.

15 <u>Her</u> is a middle school <u>student</u>.

2

다음 밑줄 친 부분들 중에서 **틀린** 곳을 바르게 고쳐 써 보자.

1 Some <u>people</u> follow <u>Tom's</u>.
  Tom

2 Is Korea <u>them</u> <u>country</u>?

3 <u>He</u> looks at <u>I</u>.

4 The pink <u>shoes</u> are <u>her</u>.

5 <u>That</u> hat is <u>he</u>.

6 <u>She</u> goes camping with <u>my sister's</u>.

7 <u>We</u> mom is an <u>artist</u>.

8 Mary and <u>hers</u> friend are wise <u>wives</u>.

9 <u>These</u> fish are <u>their</u>.

10 <u>It</u> tail is <u>long</u>.

11 <u>We</u> are in front of <u>your</u>.

12 The blue <u>jeans</u> are <u>you</u>.

13 <u>Their</u> come <u>home</u>.

14 <u>Tom</u> <u>ducks</u> are very noisy.

15 <u>Its</u> <u>sounds</u> good.

look at ~을 보다
artist 예술가
wise 현명한
tail 꼬리
in front of ~의 앞에
blue jeans 청바지
noisy 시끄러운
sound (명사) 소리
(동사) 소리나다,
~처럼 들리다

01 다음 빈칸에 들어갈 인칭대명사가 순서대로 바르게 짝지어진 것은?

• 나는 – _____
• 그의 것 – _____
• 우리들을 – _____

① me – his – our
② I – him – we
③ I – his – us
④ my – he – us
⑤ me – him – us

02 다음 우리말을 영어로 옮길 때, 빈칸에 들어갈 말로 알맞은 것은?

저 트럭들은 그들의 것이다.
→ Those trucks are _____.

① they
② their
③ them
④ theirs
⑤ ours

02
빈칸에는 they의 소유
대명사가 들어가야 한다.

03 다음 문장 중 바르지 <u>않은</u> 것은?

① This painting is her.
② Your father is a farmer.
③ We remember his face.
④ She is a kind woman.
⑤ Those books are mine.

03

painting 그림
farmer 농부
remember 기억하다

04 다음 빈칸에 들어갈 말이 순서대로 바르게 짝지어진 것은?

> _____ English teacher loves _____.
>
> _____ love him, too.

① We – our – Us
② We – us – Ours
③ Our – we – Us
④ Us – we – Our
⑤ Our – us – We

04

too ~또한, 역시

[05–06] 다음 빈칸에 들어갈 말로 알맞은 것을 고르시오.

 05

| _____ finds some treasure. |

① Her brother's
② Their
③ He
④ Our
⑤ Me

05

treasure 보물

빈칸에는 주격이와야
하고 단수 형태가
되어야 한다.

06

| Jane skates with _____. |

① us
② yours
③ he
④ their
⑤ Tom's

07 다음 중 밑줄 친 부분의 쓰임이 바르지 못한 것은?

① My father buys a car for <u>me</u>.
② <u>It</u> color is yellow.
③ These dolls are <u>my sister's</u>.
④ The policemen meet <u>them</u>.
⑤ I borrow <u>your</u> shoes.

07

borrow 빌려오다

08 다음 ( ) 안의 말을 알맞은 형태로 바꿀 때, 올바른 것끼리 짝지어진 것은?

> She buys (he) a new coat.
>
> I wait for (she).

08

buy 사다, 사주다
wait for ~를 기다리다

① he - her
② his - hers
③ him - her
④ he - she
⑤ he - hers

09 다음 빈칸에 들어갈 말로 알맞지 <u>않은</u> 것은?

> I know ＿＿＿＿＿＿＿＿＿ very well.

09

well 잘

빈칸에는 목적격이 와야
한다.

① you
② him
③ it
④ Tom
⑤ they

10 다음 밑줄 친 부분을 인칭대명사로 바르게 바꾼 것은?

> · These are <u>your dresses</u>.
>
> · Look at <u>her father</u>.

① you - he
② your - him
③ you - his
④ yours - him
⑤ yours - his

정답 및 해설 p.13

다음 빈칸에 주어진 단어를 알맞은 형태로 고쳐 써 보자.

1 He likes _____. (I)

2 These pens are _____. (we)

3 _____ name is pretty. (my friend)

4 I know _____. (he)

5 They miss _____. (she)

6 I meet _____. (they)

7 We are _____ uncles. (she)

8 _____ hands are very small. (he)

9 _____ racket is new. (Mr. William)

10 Show me _____ picture. (you)

11 It is _____. (me)

12 The bikes are _____. (we)

13 They make _____ some kites. (we)

14 He understands _____ mind. (you)

15 Tom waits for _____. (she)

Unit 07

be동사의 긍정문

be동사는 우리말의 '～이다,
～있다'의 뜻을 갖는 동사로,
주어에 따라 am, are, is로 변화한다.

Unit 07

be동사의 긍정문

be동사란?

'〜이다, 〜이 있다'의 뜻을 갖는 동사로, 주어에 따라 am, are, is로 변한다.

✛1 be동사의 의미와 형태

우리말에서는 주어에 관계없이 「〜이다, 〜이 있다」라고 말하지만, 영어에서는 주어에 따라 be동사가 am, are, is로 변화한다.

 주어 : 동작이나 상태의 주체로서 문장의 주인이며 문장 맨 앞에 온다.
동사 : 주어의 동작이나 상태를 나타내며, 주어 바로 다음에 이어서 온다.

✛2 인칭대명사 주어 + be동사

각 인칭대명사마다 be동사가 각기 다르다.

단수		복수	
I	am	We	
You	are	You	
He			are
She	is	They	
It			
Tom			

ex. I am happy.   We are happy.

You are happy.   You are happy.

He is happy.   They are happy.

She is happy.

> **Tip!** • be동사   상태를 나타내는 동사   *ex.* am, are, is
> • 일반 동사   동작/행동을 나타내는 동사   *ex.* eat, study…
> • 조동사   동사를 도와 그 동사에 어떤 특정한 의미를 보태 주는 동사   *ex.* do, can, will…

3 지시대명사 주어 + be동사

단수		복수	
This 이것은		These 이것들은	
That 저것은	is	Those 저것들은	are
It 그것은		They 그(것)들은	

주어가 단수일 때는 **is**를, 복수일 경우는 **are**를 사용한다.

ex. **This is a pencil.**   **These are pencils.**
      That is a doll.   **Those are dolls.**
      It is a ball.   **They are balls.**

 4 단수/복수명사 + be동사

단수명사		복수명사	
셀 수 없는 명사	is		are

child 어린이
missing 사라진
sour 신, 시큼한
cute 귀여운

ex. **A child is missing.**   한 아이가 없어졌다.
      The orange juice is sour.   그 오렌지 주스는 시다.

ex. **The children are cute.**   그 아이들은 귀엽다.
      Tom and his friends are happy. Tom과 그의 친구들은 기쁘다.

> **Tip!** be동사는 '～이다'와 '～있다'의 두 가지 뜻을 지닌다. be동사가 뒤에 장소와 위치를 나타내는 말과 함께 쓰
> 이면 '～있다'의 의미가 된다.
> *ex.* I am a doctor. 나는 의사이다   I am in my room. 나는 나의 방에 있다.

 5 단수형 문장을 복수형 문장으로 만들기

단수형 문장을 복수형 문장으로 만들때는 주어를 복수로, be동사도 복수형 be동사(are)
로, 보어도 복수로 만들어야 한다.

ex. I am a singer → <u>We</u> <u>are</u> <u>singers</u>.
                   주어 동사 보어

단, 보어가 형용사일 경우는 이를 복수형으로 바꿀 수 없다.

ex. He is handsome. → ~~He is handsomes.~~

다음 (   ) 안에서 알맞은 말을 골라 동그라미 해 보자.

writer 작가
painter 화가
pilot 비행사
soldier 군인
frying pan 프라이팬
dancer 무용수
honest 정직한
interesting 재미있는

1 I ((am), are, is) a writer.

2 We (am, are, is) painters.

3 It (am, are, is) a banana.

4 He (am, are, is) a pilot.

5 They (am, are, is) soldiers.

6 She (am, are, is) old.

7 Those (am, are, is) frying pans.

8 You (am, are, is) dancers.

9 Tom and Jim (am, are, is) cooks.

10 Jane (am, are, is) honest.

11 These (am, are, is) bees.

12 The game (am, are, is) very interesting.

13 The games (am, are, is) very interesting.

14 These rooms (am, are, is) clean.

15 That (am, are, is) my grandmother's sweater.

2

다음 ( ) 안에서 알맞은 말을 골라 동그라미 해 보자.

1 He (am, are, (is)) my father.

2 This (am, are, is) your hairband.

3 Those (am, are, is) hand-made.

4 You (am, are, is) clever.

5 She (am, are, is) sick.

6 They (am, are, is) vets.

7 It (am, are, is) a snake.

8 That (am, are, is) an airplane.

9 I (am, are, is) American.

10 We (am, are, is) bakers.

11 These (am, are, is) raincoats.

12 He and his wife (am, are, is) very intelligent.

13 His wife (am, are, is) very intelligent.

14 The policeman (am, are, is) brave.

15 The policemen (am, are, is) brave.

clever 영리한
sick 아픈
vet 수의사
snake 뱀
baker 제빵사
raincoat 비옷, 우비
intelligent 지적인
brave 용감한

다음 빈칸에 알맞은 be동사를 써 보자.

shoemaker 구두 만드는 사람
closed 닫힌
gentleman 신사
dragonfly 잠자리
bored 지루한
roommate 룸메이트, 방을 함께 쓰는 사람
meat 고기
dish 요리
delicious 맛있는

1 A lot of melons   *are*   on the table.

2 He   a good shoemaker.

3 The door   closed.

4 You   a gentleman.

5 Minho's brothers   young.

6 Mom   at home.

7 These   dragonflies.

8 She   a lawyer.

9 They   bears.

10 It   12 o'clock.

11 We   bored.

12 Three bottles of water   in the kitchen.

13 Tom and I   roommates.

14 This meat   delicious.

15 I   happy.

4

다음 빈칸에 알맞은 be동사를 써 보자.

1 They _are_ my aunts.

2 The jam ___ very sweet.

3 Tom and he ___ musicians.

4 The lady ___ Ben's wife.

5 The puppy and kitten ___ very small.

6 He ___ very handsome.

7 You and I ___ the same age.

8 These shirts ___ too tight for him.

9 The salad ___ salty.

10 Her hands ___ dirty.

11 Those ___ bills.

12 That ___ her hair saloon.

13 Those kangaroos ___ cute.

14 We ___ fire fighters.

15 Our living room ___ very large.

musician 음악가
same age 동갑
salad 샐러드
salty (맛이) 짠
dirty 더러운
bill 계산서
hair saloon 미용실
kangaroo 캥거루

주어진 문장을 복수형으로 만들 때, ( ) 안에서 알맞은 말을 골라 보자.

crowded 붐비는
ballerina 발레리나
thief 도둑
goat 염소

* 단수형 be동사 문장의
「주어 + be동사」를
복수형으로 바꾸는 방법
주어를 복수 형태로 바꾼다.
be동사를 복수형태
(are)로 바꾼다.

1 This watch is new.
⇨ (These watches are , These watches is) new.

2 That kite is very nice.
⇨ (Those kite are, Those kites are) very nice.

3 The lady is a model.
⇨ (The ladies is, The ladies are) models.

4 The shoe store is crowded.
⇨ (The shoe stores are, The shoe stores is) crowded.

5 I am a ballerina.
⇨ (You are, We are) ballerinas.

6 The church is big.
⇨ (The churches are, The churches is) big.

7 You are a good boy.
⇨ (You are, We are) good boys.

8 That tomato is small.
⇨ (Those tomatoes are, That tomatoes are) small.

9 The woman is a thief.
⇨ (The woman are, The women are) thieves.

10 This goat is black.
⇨ (These goats are, These goats is) black.

6

주어진 문장을 복수형으로 만들 때, ( ) 안에서 알맞은 말을 골라 보자.

1 I am a nurse.

⇨ We (are a nurses, are nurses).

2 That man is a scientist.

⇨ Those men (is scientists, are scientists).

3 This cucumber is fresh.

⇨ These cucumbers (are freshes, are fresh).

4 She is my daughter.

⇨ They (are my daughters, is my daughter).

5 This jacket is yours.

⇨ These jackets (are yours, are yourses).

6 He is a painter.

⇨ They (are a painters, are painters).

7 You are a child.

⇨ You (are childs, are children).

8 It is a wolf.

⇨ They (are wolves, is wolves).

9 This house is great.

⇨ These houses (are greats, are great).

10 That is a mouse.

⇨ Those (are mice, is mice).

---

cucumber 오이

* 단수형 be동사 문장의
「be동사 + 보어」 부분을
복수형으로 바꾸는 방법

① 보어가 셀 수 있는
명사인지 형용사인지
확인한다.

② 보어가 셀 수 있는 명사
이면, a, an을 없애고
복수형으로 바꾼다.

③ 보어가 형용사이면
복수형으로 바꾸지
않고, 그대로 둔다.

ex. She is kind.
They are
kinds. (×)

④ 보어에 소유대명사가
있을 경우에는 s를
붙이지 않도록 주의
한다.

ex. This chair is mine.
These chairs are
mines. (×)

주어진 문장을 복수형으로 만들 때, 빈칸에 알맞은 말을 써 보자.

spider 거미
light 불
wet 젖은
round 둥근
closed 닫힌

1 This is a spider.

⇨ ___These___ ___are___ spiders.

2 This light is bright.

⇨ _____ _____ bright.

3 The candy is too sour.

⇨ _____ too sour.

4 You are a pianist.

⇨ _____ pianists.

5 That bench is wet.

⇨ _____ wet.

6 I am a coach.

⇨ _____ coaches.

7 He is very tall.

⇨ _____ very tall.

8 The postman is my brother.

⇨ _____ my brothers.

9 That table is round.

⇨ _____ round.

10 This door is closed.

⇨ _____ closed.

2

주어진 문장을 복수형으로 만들 때, 빈칸에 알맞은 말을 써 보자.

1 This is an orange.

⇨ These _____ *are* _____ *oranges* _____ .

2 She is a model.

⇨ They _____ .

3 He is a policeman.

⇨ They _____ .

4 It is his.

⇨ They _____ .

5 He is busy.

⇨ They _____ .

6 That is an eraser.

⇨ Those _____ .

7 The girl is a dancer.

⇨ The girls _____ .

8 I am diligent.

⇨ We _____ .

9 The sunflower is hers.

⇨ The sunflowers _____ .

10 This koala is cute.

⇨ These koalas _____ .

tired 피곤한
eraser 지우개
diligent 부지런한
sunflower 해바라기
koala 코알라

주어진 문장을 복수형으로 바꿔 보자.

1 He is a president.

⇨ *They are presidents* .

2 This is a fish.

⇨ .

3 She is a cashier.

⇨ .

4 That dress is wonderful.

⇨ .

5 The sportsman is healthy.

⇨ .

6 This is a lion.

⇨ .

7 I am a dentist.

⇨ .

8 The fly is dirty.

⇨ .

9 This black car is mine.

⇨ .

10 It is a smart monkey.

⇨ .

president 대통령
cashier 계산원
sportsman 운동선수
healthy 건강한
dentist 치과의사
fly 파리, 날아가다
dirty 더러운

4

주어진 문장을 복수형으로 바꿔 보자.

1 It is a textbook.

⇨ *They are textbooks* .

2 This is a goose.

⇨ .

3 That lady is beautiful.

⇨ .

4 I am an artist.

⇨ .

5 This knife is sharp.

⇨ .

6 You are a writer.

⇨ .

7 That cow is hers.

⇨ .

8 This is Jane's skirt.

⇨ .

9 The room is messy.

⇨ .

10 He is an old hairdresser.

⇨ .

textbook 교과서
sharp 날카로운
writer 작가
messy 어질러진
hairdresser 미용사

주어진 주어에 맞춰 문장을 완성해 보자.

hen 암탉
housekeeper 주부
insect 곤충
fallen leaf 낙엽
eggplant 가지
barber 이발사
gentleman 신사
shining 빛나는

1 I am tired.

⇨ He   *is tired*   .

2 These hens are his.

⇨ This hen   .

3 She is a housekeeper.

⇨ They   .

4 Those are insects.

⇨ It   .

5 This is a fallen leaf.

⇨ Those   .

6 Those eggplants are sweet.

⇨ The eggplant   .

7 He is my new friend.

⇨ These   .

8 You are barbers.

⇨ He   .

9 They are gentlemen.

⇨ We   .

10 Those are very shining stars.

⇨ That   .

6

주어진 주어에 맞춰 문장을 완성해 보자.

1 Those are bears.

⇨ That _is a bear_ .

2 The man is my bodyguard.

⇨ Jack and Bill .

3 These pictures are yours.

⇨ That picture .

4 Those businessmen are free.

⇨ They .

5 You(너는) are my nephew.

⇨ You(너희들은) .

6 This is a monster.

⇨ That .

7 We are carpenters.

⇨ My father .

8 The pumpkins are yellow.

⇨ This pumpkin .

9 Those are very heavy stones.

⇨ They .

10 He is a clever boy.

⇨ These .

bodyguard 경호원
businessman 사업가
nephew 조카
monster 괴물
carpenter 목수
pumpkin 호박
stone 돌
heavy 무거운

다음 밑줄 친 부분들 중에서 틀린 곳을 바르게 고쳐 써 보자.

designer 디자이너
toothbrush 칫솔
towel 수건
lazy 게으른
soldier 군인
talented 재능있는
guitarist 기타연주자
honest 정직한
salesperson 판매원
stamp 우표
carpenter 목수

* 보어로 쓰인 형용사를
  명사로 착각하여 's'를
  붙이는 실수를 하지
  않도록 주의하자!

1 Mrs. Brown <u>are</u> a good <u>designer</u>.
     is

2 <u>Those</u> is toothbrushes.

3 She and I <u>are</u> <u>engineer</u>.

4 These <u>are</u> <u>towel</u>.

5 He and his wife <u>are</u> <u>lazys</u>.

6 The <u>young</u> man is <u>soldiers</u>.

7 He <u>am</u> a <u>pilot</u>.

8 Sujin and Mary <u>is</u> talented <u>guitarists</u>.

9 The <u>students</u> are very <u>honests</u>.

10 <u>The men</u> is a salesperson.

11 He and she <u>is</u> my <u>children</u>.

12 Those boats <u>is</u> <u>green</u>.

13 These stamps are <u>mines</u>.

14 That woman <u>are</u> <u>beautiful</u>.

15 <u>Judy and he</u> are <u>carpenter</u>.

2

다음 밑줄 친 부분들 중에서 **틀린** 곳을 바르게 고쳐 써 보자.

1 Sophia <u>are</u> my <u>niece</u>.
   is

2 He <u>is</u> a <u>postmen</u>.

3 Lilies and roses <u>are</u> beautiful <u>flower</u>.

4 The man <u>are</u> a <u>runner</u>.

5 They <u>is</u> weak <u>boys</u>.

6 You <u>is</u> <u>sick</u>.

7 <u>It</u> is a <u>chickens</u>.

8 They <u>are</u> small <u>mouse</u>.

9 <u>Those</u> is Mr. Brown's tomatoes.

10 These airplanes <u>is</u> very <u>fast</u>.

11 Joe and I <u>am</u> kind <u>helpers</u>.

12 <u>Those</u> are sweet <u>peach</u>.

13 This <u>is</u> her <u>rings</u>.

14 Jinsu <u>are</u> <u>strong</u>.

15 These <u>raincoat</u> are <u>wet</u>.

niece 여자조카
runner 달리기 선수
weak 약한
sick 아픈
helper 도우미
ring 반지
raincoat 비옷
wet 젖은

01 다음 중 주어와 동사의 연결이 <u>잘못된</u> 것은?

① I - am
② You - are
③ She - is
④ We - am
⑤ They - are

02 다음 빈칸에 들어갈 말로 알맞은 것은?

Those _____ small donkeys.

① is   ② are
③ am   ④ an
⑤ do

02

donkey 당나귀

03 다음 빈칸에 is를 쓸 수 <u>없는</u> 것은?

① The cat _____ poor.
② Judy _____ a runner.
③ My brothers _____ busy.
④ The student _____ tall.
⑤ That boy _____ American.

03

busy 바쁜

04 다음 빈칸에 공통으로 들어갈 말로 알맞은 것은?

> · They _____ cooks.
>
> · My uncles _____ scientists.

① am   ② are
③ is   ④ the
⑤ a

05 다음 중 be동사의 사용이 바른 것은?

① My grandparents is very old.
② I are a middle school student.
③ John and Mary is good swimmers.
④ These cars is expensive.
⑤ She is a dentist.

04
주어가 모두 복수이다

05

kindergarten 유치원
elementary school
초등학교
middle school 중학교
high school 고등학교
university [college]
대학교
expensive 값비싼
dentist 치과의사

실전Test

06 다음 빈칸에 들어갈 말이 순서대로 바르게 짝지어진 것은?

> • You _____ a lazy girl.
>
> • These _____ soft erasers.

① are - are   ② is - are
③ am - is   ④ are - am
⑤ is - is

07 다음 문장 중 바르지 <u>않은</u> 것은?

① Minji is Korean.
② That blanket is white.
③ Jane and I am elementary school students.
④ It is a funny movie.
⑤ This room is clean.

08 다음 중 밑줄 친 부분의 의미가 <u>다른</u> 것은?

① Susan <u>is</u> at school.
② Judy <u>is</u> a smart student.
③ It <u>is</u> an easy storybook.
④ He <u>is</u> a tall boy.
⑤ She <u>is</u> a science teacher.

06
lazy 게으른
eraser 지우개

07
blanket 담요
funny 재미있는
clean 깨끗한

08
smart 영리한
storybook 이야기책
science 과학

be동사는 '~이다'와
'~있다'의 두 가지
의미를 지닌다.

09

gooding–looking
잘생긴

09 다음 우리말을 영어로 옮길 때, 빈칸에 알맞은 말을 쓰시오.

> 민수와 수빈이는 매우 잘생겼다.
>
> → Minsu and Subin _____ very good-looking.

10 다음 빈칸에 들어갈 말로 알맞은 것은?

> _____ is beautiful.

① You
② They
③ The ladies
④ My sisters
⑤ The girl

Quiz!

다음 ( ) 안에 알맞은 be동사를 써 보자.

1 That knife _____ very sharp.

2 She _____ a very fast woman.

3 The horses _____ white.

4 These mice _____ big.

5 The children _____ happy.

주어진 문장을 복수형 문장으로 만들어 보자.

1 This is a strong ox.

   ⇨ _____ .

2 I am too late.

   ⇨ _____ .

3 She is a singer.

   ⇨ _____ .

4 His shirt is colorful.

   ⇨ _____ .

5 It is a yellow umbrella.

   ⇨ _____ .

Unit 08

be동사의
부정문, 의문문

be동사의 부정문은
「주어 + be동사 + not~」의 순서로 쓰고,
의문문은 「be동사 + 주어~?」의
순서로 쓴다.

Unit 08

be동사의 부정문, 의문문

1 be동사의 부정문

be동사 바로 뒤에 **not**만 붙이면 된다.

ex. I am not a student.　　　　나는 학생이 아니다.
You are not my teacher.　당신은 나의 선생님이 아니다.
He is not kind.　　　　　그는 친절하지 않다.
She is not pretty.　　　　그녀는 예쁘지 않다.

2 be동사의 의문문

be동사와 주어의 위치를 바꾸고, 문장 마지막에 물음표(?)를 붙인다.

☐ You are a teacher.

ex. **Are you** a teacher?　너는 선생님이니?

3 be동사의 의문문의 대답

Yes나 No 그리고 be동사를 이용해서 대답하고 주어는 대명사로 받는다. 단, 질문하는 사람과 대답하는 사람의 입장에 따라 질문의 주어와 대답의 주어가 달라질 수 있는 것에 주의한다.

인칭대명사의 대답

- 나는(I)으로 물어보면 너는(you)으로 대답한다.
- 우리들은(we)으로 물어보면 너희들은(you)으로 대답한다.
- 그는(he), 그녀는(she)으로 물어보면 그는(he), 그녀는(she)로 대답한다.
- 그들은(they)로 물어보면 그들은(they)로 대답한다.
- 너는(you)으로 물어보면 나는(I)으로 대답한다.
- 너희들은(you)으로 물어보면 우리는(we)으로 대답한다.

단수		복수	
질문	대답	질문	대답
Am I ~?	~, you are (not).	Are we ~?	~, you are (not).
Are you ~?	~, I am (not).	Are you ~?	~, we are (not).
Is he ~?	~, he is (not).	Are they ~?	~, they are (not).
Is she ~?	~, she is (not).		
Is it ~?	~, it is (not).		

ex. Are **you** happy? 너는 행복하니?
    Yes, **I am** (happy). 네, 그래요.
    No, **I am not** (happy). 아니요, 그렇지 않아요.

지시대명사의 대답
- 이것(this), 저것(that), 그것(it)으로 물어 보면 모두 그것(it)으로 대답한다.
- 이것들(these), 저것들(those), 그것들(they)로 물어 보면 모두 그것들(they)로 대답한다.

단수		복수	
질문	대답	질문	대답
Is this ~?	~, it is (not).	Are these ~?	~, they are (not).
Is that ~?		Are those ~?	

ex. Is **this** your book? 이것은 너의 책이니?
    긍정 – **Yes, it is** (mine). 응, 그래. 부정 – **No, It is not** (mine). 아니, 그렇지 않아.

> **Tip!** 우리들은(we)으로 물어보는 경우 상황에 따라 we에 '나' 자신도 포함되어 있는 경우에는 우리들은(we)으로 답할 수 있다.

1 축약형 만들기
축약형이란 간단히 줄여서 쓰는 형태를 말하며, 두 단어를 한 단어로 줄이기 위해서 철자 하나를 빼고 생략부호(')로 대신한다.

▶ 대명사 주어 + be동사

I	+ am	I'm	He		He's
You		You're	She		She's
We	+ are	We're	It	+ is	It's
They		They're	That		That's

▶ be동사 + not

are	+ not	aren't	is	+ not	isn't

* This+ is, am+not 은 축약형을 만들지 않는다. *ex.* ~~This's, amn't~~

No로 대답할 경우,   No, I'm not. No, you're not. 등과 같이 축약형을 사용하기도 하지만
Yes로 대답할 경우에는   ~~Yes, I'm.~~ ~~Yes, you're.~~ 등 처럼 축약형을 사용하지 않는다.

다음 두 단어의 축약형을 써 보자.

1   I   +   am   =   *I'm*

2   are   +   not   =

3   She   +   is   =

4   is   +   not   =

5   You   +   are   =

6   It   +   is   =

7   That   +   is   =

8   We   +   are   =

9   They   +   are   =

10   He   +   is   =

2

주어진 문장을 부정문으로 만들어 보세요.

1 I am Jinho.

⇨   *I'm*   *not*   Jinho.

2 She is my niece.

⇨   my niece.

3 They are camels.

⇨   camels.

4 He is a famous painter.

⇨   a famous painter.

5 We are free.

⇨   free.

6 You are a vet.

⇨   a vet.

7 That is a bowl.

⇨   a bowl.

8 It is a lily.

⇨   a lily.

9 She is my tutor.

⇨   my tutor.

10 You are pretty.

⇨   pretty.

niece (여자)조카
camel 낙타
painter 화가
vet 수의사
bowl 사발
tutor 개인 지도 교사

주어진 문장을 의문문으로 바꿔 보자.

baker 제빵사
giraffe 기린
jacket 재킷, 웃옷
bicycle 자전거
lipstick 립스틱

1 I am pretty.

   – _Am_   _I_   pretty?

2 You are an English teacher.

   –   an English teacher?

3 He is a baker.

   –   a baker?

4 Mary is kind.

   –   kind?

5 You are Koreans.

   –   Koreans?

6 The giraffe is very tall.

   –   very tall?

7 That is a yellow jacket.

   –   a yellow jacket?

8 that biciycle이 주어

8 She is a pretty girl.

   –   a pretty girl?

9 They are your friend.

   –   your friend?

10 These are her lipsticks.

   –   her lipsticks?

4

다음 문장을 지시대로 바꿔 보자.

1 I am late for school.

의문문   *Am*   *I*   late for school?

2 They are cooks.

부정문   cooks.

3 It is your puppy.

의문문   your puppy?

4 We are her friends.

부정문   her friends.

5 She is ill.

의문문   ill?

6 He is hungry.

부정문   hungry.

7 His concert is wonderful.

의문문   wonderful?

8 The woman is very famous.

부정문   very famous.

9 Jane's hair is short.

의문문   short?

10 This is dirty.

부정문   dirty.

late 늦은
cook 요리사
famous 유명한

다음 질문에 대한 Yes 또는 No의 대답을 완성해 보자.

math 수학
coach 코치

* 'I'로 물으면 'you'로 대답
하고, 단수 'you'로 물으면
'I'로 대답하며 복수 'you'
(너희들)로 물으면 'we'로
대답한다.

1 Am I your math teacher?

– Yes, *you* *are* .

Are we your math teachers?

– Yes, .

2 Are you a coach?

– No, .

Are you coaches?

– Yes, .

3 Is this a chair?

– Yes, .

Are these chairs?

– No, .

4 Is that a new computer?

– Yes, .

Are those new computers?

– Yes, .

5 Are you a singer?

– No, .

Are you singers?

– Yes, .

6 Is it a pig?

– No, .

Are they pigs?

– Yes, .

2

다음 질문에 대한 Yes 또는 No의 대답을 완성해 보자.

1 Is he a handsome guy?

- Yes, *he* *is* .

Are they handsome guys?

- Yes, .

2 Is the window open?

- Yes, .

Are the windows open?

- Yes, .

3 Is Inho an honest boy?

- Yes, .

Are they honest boys?

- No, .

4 Is this cookie delicious?

- Yes, .

Are these cookies delicious?

- No, .

5 Am I late?

- No, .

Are we late?

- Yes, .

6 Are you a basketball player?

- No, .

Are you basketball players?

- Yes, .

guy 남자
delicious 맛있는
basketball 농구

다음 질문에 대한 Yes 또는 No의 대답을 완성해 보자.

present 선물
painting 그림
daugther 딸

1 Is that present mine?

– Yes, _It_ is _yours_ .

2 Are these cars yours (너의 것)?

– Yes, _____ _____ mine.

3 Is she his mother?

– Yes, _____ _____ .

4 Is that painting his?

– Yes, _____ _____ his.

5 Are the desks ours?

– Yes, _____ are _____ .

6 Is this my toy?

– Yes, _____ . It is _____ toy.

7 Are those girls her daughters?

– No, _____ _____ .

8 Is Tommy your (너희들의) brother?

– Yes, _____ is _____ brother.

9 Are these pineapples hers?

– No, _____ not.

10 Are those our crayons?

– Yes, _____ are _____ crayons.

4

다음 질문에 대한 Yes 또는 No의 대답을 완성해 보자.

1 Are those ribbons yours (너희들의 것)?

– Yes, *they* **are** *ours* .

2 Is the lawyer her sister?

– No, her sister.

3 Is this sweater his?

– No, isn't .

4 Are these carrots the farmer's?

– Yes, they .

5 Is that your (너의) school?

– Yes, is. is school.

6 Are those young men his cousins?

– Yes, his cousins.

7 Is this Mary's office?

– No, it .

8 Are they my necklaces?

– Yes, are. They are necklaces.

9 Are those sheep Paul's?

– Yes, they are. are .

10 Are these our CDs?

– No, they CDs.

lawyer 변호사
sweater 스웨터
carrot 당근
cousin 사촌
office 사무실

* 단수 this, that, it으로
물으면 it으로 대답하고,
복수 these, those,
they로 물으면 they로
대답한다.

다음 문장에서 밑줄 친 부분을 바르게 고쳐 써 보자.

meeting 회의
cellist 첼로 연주자
button 단추
salesperson 영업 사원
basket 바구니
unkind 불친절한

1 Is this a kiwi?   – Yes, <u>this is</u>.
it

2 I <u>are</u> free.

3 Is she Mary?   – Yes, <u>she's</u>.

4 My husband and Tom <u>isn't</u> angry.

5 Are you cellists?   – Yes, <u>you are</u>.

6 Those <u>is</u> buttons.

7 Are you (너는) happy?   – No, <u>we aren't</u>.

8 It <u>aren't</u> fine.

9 John and Tom <u>is</u> brave soldiers.

10 Are the students kind to the boy?   – Yes, <u>he is</u>.

11 You <u>isn't</u> salespersons.

12 <u>Is</u> these her baskets?

13 Am I unkind?   – No, <u>I'm not</u>.

14 <u>Are</u> Mary too sick?

15 Are you a model?   – No, <u>we're</u> not.

2

다음 문장에서 밑줄 친 부분을 바르게 고쳐 써 보자.

1 Are these comic books fun?   – Yes, <u>these</u> are.
                                            they

2 Are you good students?   – Yes, <u>I am</u>.

3 Is he your brother?   – Yes, he <u>is not</u>.

4 Is your dog smart?   – Yes, <u>it's</u>.

5 She and I <u>not are</u> his old friends.

6 Are you baseball players?   – No, <u>we are</u>.

7 My mother <u>not is</u> a kind woman.

8 Are your brothers clever?   – Yes, <u>he is</u>.

9 Am I good-looking?   – Yes, <u>I am</u>.

10 Are your sisters pretty girls?   – Yes, <u>they're</u>.

11 Are they rich men?   – Yes, <u>he is</u>.

12 Is that your pencil case?   – Yes, <u>that</u> is.

13 Is this worm an insect?   – No, <u>this</u> is not.

14 Are those his cars?   – No, <u>those aren't</u>.

15 Are you a firefighter?   – No, <u>we aren't</u>.

comic book 만화책
excellent 아주 훌륭한
good-looking 잘생긴
worm 벌레
insect 곤충
fire fighter 소방관

01 다음 문장에서 not이 들어가기에 알맞은 곳은?

> This ① is ② a ③ very ④ fantastic ⑤ picture.

01
fantastic 환상적인

be동사의 부정문은
be동사 바로 뒤에
not을 붙인다.

[02-03] 다음 중 물음에 대한 대답이 바르지 <u>않은</u> 것을 고르시오.

02
① Is this an umbrella?   – Yes, it is.
② Are you a singer?   – No, I'm not.
③ Are they pigs?   – Yes, they are.
④ Is the window open?   – Yes, it is.
⑤ Are you a fisherman?   – Yes, you are.

02
you(단수)로 물어 보면
I로 대답한다.

03
① Is the horse hungry?   – Yes, it is.
② Is she a singer?   – No, she isn't.
③ Are they koreans?   – Yes, they are.
④ Are the buildings high?   – Yes, it is.
⑤ Is he sick?   – Yes, he is.

04 다음 문장을 의문문과 부정문으로 바꿔 쓰시오.

> Your uncle is diligent.

의문문 : _____

부정문 : _____

정답 및 해설 p.16

05 다음 중 바르지 않은 것을 고르면?

① Yes, I am.
② No, they're not.
③ Yes, she's.
④ No, he's not.
⑤ No, it's not.

06 다음 대답이 나올 수 있는 물음으로 알맞은 것은?

> A : _____
> B : Yes, we are.

① Is he a doctor?　　② Am I a doctor?
③ Are you a doctor?　④ Are they doctors?
⑤ Are you doctors?

07 다음 중 축약형이 바르지 <u>않은</u> 것은?

① I'm
② She's
③ We're
④ This's
⑤ That's

08 다음 대화의 빈칸에 들어갈 말로 알맞은 것은?

A : Is that his new cello?

B : _____

① Yes, that is.
② No, that isn't.
③ Yes, it is.
④ Yes, he is.
⑤ No, he isn't.

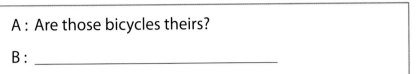

09 다음 대화에서 물음에 대한 대답으로 알맞은 것은? (2개)

> A : Are those bicycles theirs?
>
> B : _____

① Yes, those are.
② No, these aren't.
③ Yes, they are.
④ They are theirs.
⑤ No, they aren't.

09

those로 물어 보면 they로 대답하고 be동사로 시작한 질문은 'yes' 또는 'no'로 대답한다.

정답 및 해설 p.16

10 다음 빈칸에 들어갈 말로 알맞은 것은?

> A : Are you Mr. Park?
>
> B : _____

① Yes, you are.
② Yes, I am.
③ No, I am.
④ No, you aren't.
⑤ Yes, he is.

10

you로 물어보면 단수일 때는 I로, 복수일 때는 we로 대답한다.

다음 문장을 지시대로 바꿔 써 보자.

1 You are hungry.

의문문

2 The boy is very kind.

부정문

3 They are singers.

의문문

4 It is his digital camera.

부정문

5 Those erasers are yours.

의문문

다음 물음에 대한 Yes 또는 No의 대답을 완성해 보자.

1 Are you her brother?

Yes,   .

2 Are those books ours?

Yes,   .

3 Is that Tom's?

No,   .

4 Are you designers?

Yes,   .

5 Is Paul busy?

No,   .

- Review Test 2
- 내신대비 2

01   다음 (   ) 안에서 알맞은 말을 골라 동그라미 해 보자.

1   (This, These) are cows.

2   (I, We) are police officers.

3   (They, It) are my dogs.

4   (That, Those) is a bug.

5   (You, She) are kind nurses.

6   (They, He) is my dad.

7   (This, These) are pilots.

02   주어진 단어의 알맞은 형태를 써 보자.

1   _____ is my aunt. (she)

2   _____ are good boys. (he)

3   _____ are young people. (you)

4   _____ is his hat. (this)

5   _____ are my pigs. (that)

6   _____ are best singers. (I)

7   _____ is a nice car. (it)

03 다음을 복수형으로 바르게 바꾼 것을 골라 ○표 해 보자.

1 the tiger   (the tigers, they tigers, they tiger)

2 this hen   (these hen, this hens, these hens)

3 that bed   (that beds, those beds, those bed)

4 the baby   (these baby, the babies, they babies)

5 that child   (those children, that children, those childs)

6 the photo   (these photos, the photoes, the photos)

7 this coat   (this coats, these coat, these coats)

04 다음을 복수형으로 바꿔 써 보자.

1 that boy

2 this mouse

3 the leaf

4 that house

5 this hamburger

6 the strawberry

7 that dish

01 빈칸을 채워 인칭대명사의 격변화와 소유대명사를 완성해 보자.

종류		주격	소유격	목적격	소유대명사
단수	1인칭	I 나는	나의	나를(에게)	나의 것
	2인칭	you 너는	너의	너를(에게)	너의 것
	3인칭	he 그는	그의	그를(에게)	그의 것
		she 그녀는	그녀의	그녀를(에게)	그녀의 것
		it 그것은	그것의	그것을(에게)	– –
복수	1인칭	we 우리들은	우리들의	우리들을(에게)	우리들의 것
	2인칭	you 너희들은	너희들의	너희들을	너희들의 것
	3인칭	they 그(것)들은	그(것)들의	그(것)들을(에게)	그들의 것
의문사 who		who 누가	누구의	누구를(에게)	누구의 것

02 빈칸을 채워 명사의 격변화와 소유대명사를 완성해 보자.

종류	주격	소유격	목적격	소유대명사
고유명사	Tom Tom은	Tom의	Tom을(에게)	Tom의 것
보통명사	my sister 나의 여동생은	나의 여동생의	나의 여동생을(에게)	나의 여동생의 것

정답 및 해설 p.17

03 다음 빈칸에 알맞은 인칭대명사를 써 보자.

1 그녀의

2 나의 것

3 나를(에게)

4 우리들의

5 Tom의 것

6 나의 여동생을(에게)

7 그의

8 너희들의 것

9 그것의

10 그들의 것

11 너희들의

12 그를(에게)

13 우리들의 것

14 그녀의 것

04 다음 빈칸에 ( ) 안의 대명사를 알맞은 형태로 고쳐 써 보자.

1 I know _____. (he)

2 Her dad loves _____. (she)

3 He meets _____ everyday. (we)

4 This bag is _____. (I)

5 My mom takes care of _____. (they)

6 Jane sometimes uses _____ computer. (Tom)

7 _____ eyes are red. (it)

01 다음 ( ) 안에서 알맞은 말을 골라 동그라미 해 보자.

1 She (am , are, is) my sister.

2 That (am , are, is) your book.

3 These flowers (am , are, is) tulips.

4 He and his brother (am , are, is) smart.

5 John (am , are, is) a salesperson. salesperson 판매원

6 This (am , are, is) a very long train.

7 We (am , are, is) workers.

8 It (am , are, is) my laptop computer. laptop computer 노트북

9 (Am , Are, Is) you from China?

10 The girl (am, are, is) beautiful.

11 Those (am, are, is) old game CDs.

12 He and his wife (am, are, is) very famous.

13 The woman (am, are, is) on the street.

14 These cartoons (am, are, is) very exciting. cartoon 만화

15 I (am, are, is) too lazy.

O2 다음 빈칸에 알맞은 be동사를 써 보자.

1 A lot of water   in the pond.

2 He   a great musician. musician 음악가

3 Sumi and Ann   at the bank. bank 은행

4 Jane   in blue. be in blue 우울하다

5 They   young people.

6 The dog   on the sofa.

7 These   white butterflies. butterfly 나비

8 She   a nurse.

9 They   wild animals.

10 Those balls   red.

11 We   bored. bored 지루한

12 Where   Miss. Kim?

13 I   in the restaurant.

14 His cousins   studios. studios 공부를 좋아하는

15 We   good teachers.

01 다음 문장을 지시대로 바꿔 보자.

1 I am tall.

부정문 _____ tall.

2 They are full.

의문문 _____ full?

3 It is a good question.

의문문 _____ a good question?

4 We are hungry.

부정문 _____ hungry.

5 She is my cousin.

부정문 _____ my cousin.

6 Jane is angry.

의문문 _____ angry?

7 Here is a small town.

부정문 _____ a small town.

8 Your sister is very famous.

의문문 _____ very famous?

9 Those paintings are Picasso's.

부정문 _____ Picasso's.

10 Tom and John are the same age.

의문문 _____ the same age?

O2 다음 질문에 대한 대답을 완성해 보자.

1 Is he a ballerina?

– Yes,

2 Are you(너는) bored?

– No,

3 Am I slim?

– Yes,

4 Are those sweaters hand-made ?

– No,

5 Are you(너희들은) Koreans?

– No,

6 Is it yours?

– Yes,

7 Is this a brand new car. brand new 신형의

– No,

8 Is your mom sick?

– Yes,

9 Are these his ties? tie 넥타이

– Yes,

10 Are they in the library?

– No,

01 다음 밑줄 친 곳에 공통으로 들어갈 알맞은 것은?

> _____ are a nurse.
>
> _____ are nurses.

① I
② You
③ She
④ We
⑤ They

02 다음 문장 중 어법상 옳은 것 두 개를 고르면?

① These is a pencil.
② These are a pencil.
③ Those are pencils.
④ Those is a pencils.
⑤ They are pencils.

03 다음 밑줄 친 것을 받아줄 대명사로 짝지어진 것은?

> Tom and I are soldiers.
> _____ are brave.
> Tom and you are kind.
> _____ are nice.

① They – We
② You – They
③ We – They
④ We – You
⑤ They – We

04 다음 밑줄 친 곳에 들어갈 대명사는?

> *Jenny* : The bride is so beautiful.
> *Mary* : _____ is my sister.

bride 신부

① He
② You
③ She
④ We
⑤ They

05 지시대명사를 두 개를 고르면?

① <u>This</u> book is mine.
② <u>These</u> dolls are very cute.
③ <u>That</u> house is wonderful.
④ <u>Those</u> are his dogs.
⑤ <u>They</u> are little boys.

08 다음 중 어법상 옳은 것은?

① I like he.
② He invites my.
③ His cat is black.
④ She finds hers schoolbag.
⑤ Their go swimming.

invite 초대하다

06 복수형으로 바꿀 때 밑줄 친 곳에 들어갈 말로 옳은 것은?

> that computer -
> _____ computers

① this
② these
③ the
④ those
⑤ they

09 밑줄친 곳에 주어진 대명사의 알맞은 격을 써 보세요.

> This is _____ classroom.
> (we)

classroom 교실

07 다음 중 단수형과 복수형이 바르게 짝지어 진 것은?

① this baby - these babies
② this lady - this ladies
③ that apple - thoses apples
④ the book - they books
⑤ this CD - those CDs

10 밑줄친 곳에 들어갈 알맞은 것은?

> Tom meets _____.
> He looks at _____ doll.

① her - her
② she - her
③ them - they
④ it - its
⑤ our - us

11 다음 중 her가 들어갈 수 없는 곳을 골라 보세요.

① I love _____.
② _____ sister is very pretty.
③ _____ calls me every day.
④ He knows _____ mother.
⑤ Tom visits _____.

visit 방문하다

12 다음 중 어법상 옳지 않은 것은?

① God loves us.
② Who is your teacher?
③ Their cars are at the parking lot.
④ I call Jane's everyday.
⑤ Her dress is beautiful.

13 밑줄 친 곳에 들어갈 것은?

She _____ happy.
He and she _____ so nice.

① is - is
② am - is
③ are - is
④ is - are
⑤ are - are

14 다음 중 밑줄 친 곳에 공통으로 들어갈 수 있는 것은?

We _____ too sad.
The girls _____ beautiful.

① am
② are
③ is

15 다음 중 어법상 옳지 않은 것은?

① The foxes are hungry.
② He and I am tired.
③ The woman is too fat.
④ They are your brothers.
⑤ That is an old bus.

16 주어진 문장을 복수형 문장으로 올바르게 바꾼 것은?

> This is her cat.

① This is her cats.
② These is her cat.
③ These is her cat.
④ These are her cats.
⑤ These is her cats.

17 주어진 문장을 부정문과 의문문으로 바꿔 보세요 .

> They are good - looking.

부정문 : _____

의문문 : _____

18 주어진 질문에 알맞은 답을 두 개를 고르면?

> Are you at home?

① Yes, you are.
② No, you aren't.
③ Yes, I am.
④ Yes, I am not.
⑤ No, I'm not.

19 밑줄 친 곳에 공통으로 들어갈 알맞은 것을 고르면?

> Are those your socks?
> No, _____ aren't.
> Are these glasses his?
> No, _____ aren't.
> Are they hers?
> No, _____ aren't.

① they
② these
③ those
④ that
⑤ this

20 다음 밑줄 친 부분을 바르게 고쳐 써 보세요.

> Are you engineers?
> – Yes, I <u>am</u>.

_____

engineer 기술자

21 다음 문장의 주어를 아래와 같이 바꿀 때 문장을 완성해 보세요.

They are good boys.

⇨ He _____

22 빈칸에 알맞은 be동사를 써 보세요.

Jane's brother _____ at the desk.
Jane _____ in the library.
Jane and Jane's sister _____at the mall.

library 도서관

23 다음 중 a를 붙일 수 <u>없는</u> 것 둘을 고르면?

① lion
② table
③ rose
④ Korea
⑤ water

24 다음 빈칸에 들어갈 것은?

Is she a pianist?
– Yes, _____ is.
Is he a swimmer?
– Yes, _____ is.
Are he and she pilots?
– No, _____ aren't.

① it - she - he
② she - he -she
③ you - he -he
④ she - he - you
⑤ she - he -they

pilot 조종사

25 다음 중 어법상 옳지 <u>않은</u> 것 두개를 고르세요.

① He and she is my friends.
② I am her teacher.
③ We are his parents.
④ Those apple are fresh.
⑤ Jane is kind.

fresh 신선한

1·2회

종합문제

01 다음 중 es를 붙여 명사의 복수형을 만드는 것은? (2개)

① piano
② roof
③ dish
④ desk
⑤ potato

02 다음 중 바르지 않은 것은?

① two knives
② three children
③ six students
④ ten oxen
⑤ two chair

03 다음 명사의 복수형을 쓰시오.

leaf – _____

04 다음 중 복수형과 단수형이 바르게 짝지어 지지 않은 것은?

복수형	단수형
① men	– man
② cars	– car
③ lilies	– lily
④ classmates	– classmat
⑤ geese	– goose

05 다음 중 단수형과 복수형이 바르게 짝지어 지지 않은 것은?

단수형	복수형
① tooth	– teeth
② fish	– fish
③ toy	– toys
④ mouse	– mouses
⑤ woman	– women

06 다음 중 셀 수 없는 명사가 아닌 것은?

① bicycle
② butter
③ milk
④ gas
⑤ gold

07 다음 우리말을 영어로 쓸 때, 빈칸에 알맞은 말을 쓰시오.

> - 옥수수 3캔
>   three _____ of corn
> - 주스 2팩
>   two _____ of juice

08 다음 빈칸에 공통으로 들어갈 말을 쓰시오.

> - a _____ of cake
> - a _____ of pizza
> - a _____ of paper
> - a _____ of advice

_____

09 다음은 욕실에 있는 물건들이다. 빈칸에 들어갈 말이 순서대로 바르게 짝지어진 것은?

> - five _____ of soap
> - a _____ of shampoo
> - two _____ of toothpaste

① bar – bottles – tube
② bars – bottle – tube
③ bar – bottle – tubes
④ bars – bottle – tubes
⑤ bars – bottles – tube

10 다음 중 밑줄 친 ①~③ 중에서 틀린 것을 바르게 고쳐 쓰시오.

> Tom eats four ① loaf of bread, six ② cans of Coke and three ③ bunches of bananas every day. He is very fat.

_____ ⇨ _____

11 다음 중 관사가 잘못 쓰인 것은?

① a exciting game
② a pretty girl
③ an easy book
④ a fresh apple
⑤ an honest man

12 다음 빈칸에 들어갈 말이 순서대로 바르게 짝지어진 것은?

> _____ monkey is in the zoo. _____ monkey is small. It comes from _____ Africa.

① A - A - the
② The - An - a
③ A - The - 필요없음
④ The - The - a
⑤ A - 필요없음 - the

[13–14] 다음 문장 중 바른 것을 고르시오.

13
① A moon is between an earth and a sun.
② The moon is between the earth and a sun.
③ A moon is between an earth and the sun.
④ The moon is between the earth and the sun.
⑤ The moon is between an earth and the sun.

14
① I have the dinner at 7.
② It is a my father's car.
③ My sister plays the violin.
④ He stays in Hyatt Hotel.
⑤ Tommy plays the soccer.

15 다음 중 'a'가 들어갈 수 없는 곳을 모두 고르면?

I see ⓐ beautiful woman at the store. She has ⓑ long hair. She wears ⓒ red dress. I remember her. She is ⓓ my teacher.

① ⓐ, ⓑ
② ⓐ, ⓒ
③ ⓑ, ⓒ
④ ⓑ, ⓓ
⑤ ⓐ, ⓓ

16 다음 빈칸에 들어갈 말로 알맞지 않은 것은?

_____ is a very diligent farmer.

① He
② Judy
③ Andy
④ Tom and Paul
⑤ Mr. Smith

17 다음 문장에서 <u>틀린</u> 부분을 찾아 바르게 고쳐 쓰시오.

| He is a computer programmers. |

_____ ⇨ _____

18 다음 문장을 복수형으로 바꿀 때, 빈칸에 공통으로 들어갈 말로 알맞은 것은?

| · She is a pianist. |
| → _____ are pianists. |
| · He is kind. |
| → _____ are kind. |

① We
② You
③ They
④ These
⑤ Those

19 다음 빈칸에 들어갈 말로 알맞지 <u>않은</u> 것은?

| _____ are taxi drivers. |

① Susie and Bob
② You
③ We
④ The old man
⑤ My uncles

20 다음 밑줄 친 문장을 복수형으로 바꿔 쓰시오.

| I have two dogs.
| <u>It is a wonderful pet.</u>
| I love them. |

_____

01 다음 밑줄 친 부분 중 성격이 <u>다른</u> 것은?

① <u>This</u> book is very easy.
② <u>Those</u> oranges are sweet.
③ <u>That</u> is my ball.
④ <u>These</u> desks are old.
⑤ <u>That</u> child is my brother.

02 다음 문장 중 바른 것은?

① Those mouse is very fast.
② These glass are clean.
③ Those child is smart.
④ These train are long.
⑤ Those cookies are sweet.

03 다음 빈칸에 들어갈 말이 순서대로 바르게 짝지어진 것은?

> · _____ nurses are kind.
> · _____ computer is new.

① This - That
② This - Those
③ These - Those
④ These - That
⑤ The - These

04 다음 문장을 단수형으로 바꿔 쓸 때, 빈칸에 알맞은 말을 쓰시오.

> We are doctors.
> → _____ am a doctor.

05 다음 문장을 복수형으로 바꿔 쓸 때, 빈칸에 들어갈 말로 알맞은 것은?

> The roof is green.
> → _____ are green.

① These roofs
② Those roofs
③ That roofs
④ This roof
⑤ The roofs

06 다음 우리말에 해당하는 인칭대명사가 순서대로 바르게 짝지어진 것은?

> • 너는   – _____
>
> • 그녀의   – _____
>
> • 그들을   – _____

① you - hers - their
② you - her - them
③ you - she - theirs
④ you - hers - they
⑤ you - hers - them

07 다음 밑줄 친 부분 중 바른 것은?

① That computer is <u>me</u>.
② <u>Your</u> friend is good.
③ <u>We</u> bags are big.
④ She loves <u>he</u>.
⑤ This dress is <u>my sister</u>.

08 다음 빈칸에 들어갈 말이 순서대로 바르게 짝지어진 것은?

> • Jane gives _____ a book.
>
> • Tom always looks for _____.

① me – we
② my – us
③ me – our
④ me – us
⑤ I – we

09 다음 우리말을 영어로 바꿔 쓸 때, 틀린 부분을 찾아 바르게 고쳐 쓰시오.

> 이 장난감들은 그의 것이다.
>
> → These toys are him.

_____ ⇨ _____

10 다음 밑줄 친 부분 중 쓰임이 다른 것은?

① That is <u>Tom's</u> ball.
② It's my <u>father's</u> car.
③ This piano is <u>Maria's</u>.
④ They are <u>Sumi's</u> friends.
⑤ This is <u>Jane's</u> ruler.

11 다음 빈칸에 is가 들어갈 수 <u>없는</u> 것은?

① That _____ an airplane.
② His sister _____ very kind.
③ Minho's brothers _____ young.
④ It _____ 9 o'clock.
⑤ This cheese _____ yellow.

12 다음 빈칸에 들어갈 말이 순서대로 바르게 짝 지어진 것은?

> · We _____ bakers.
> · Her son _____ smart.

① is – are
② are – are
③ am – are
④ is – am
⑤ are – is

13 다음 중 축약형이 바르지 <u>않은</u> 것은?

① I + am → I'm
② they + are → they're
③ she + is → she's
④ it + is → its
⑤ are + not → aren't

14 다음 빈칸에 들어갈 말이 순서대로 바르게 짝지어진 것은?

> · It _____ hot today.
> · Two bottles _____ red.
> · Sugar _____ sweet.

① are – are – are
② is – are – is
③ is – is – are
④ are – are – is
⑤ is – are – are

15 다음 중 밑줄 친 is의 뜻이 <u>다른</u> 것은?

① That <u>is</u> a beautiful doll.
② She <u>is</u> a famous pianist.
③ Tom <u>is</u> in his room.
④ My mother <u>is</u> a teacher.
⑤ It <u>is</u> a very cute puppy.

16 다음 문장을 의문문과 부정문으로 바꿔 쓰시오.

> Seoul is your hometown.

의문문 : _____

부정문 : _____

17 다음 빈칸에 들어갈 말로 알맞은 것은?

> A : Is this schoolbag yours?
> B : _____. It's my
>   brother's.

① Yes, it is.
② No, I'm not.
③ Yes, this is.
④ No, it isn't.
⑤ No, this isn't.

18 다음 빈칸에 들어갈 말이 순서대로 바르게 짝
지어진 것은?

> Sora : Is your wife healthy?
> Kevin : Yes, _____ is.
> Sora : That sounds good.
> Kevin : How about you? Are you
>   healthy?
> Sora : No, _____.

① I – I'm not
② you – you're not
③ she – I'm not
④ they – I'm not
⑤ she – you're not

19 다음 빈칸에 들어갈 말로 알맞지 <u>않은</u> 것은?

> _____
> – Yes, they are.

① Are these apples?
② Are Bill and Jack angry?
③ Are they swimmers?
④ Are you late for the concert?
⑤ Are those umbrellas yours?

20 다음 중 물음과 대답이 바르지 <u>않은</u> 것은?

① Is the girl tall?
  – Yes, she is.
② Is your brother sick?
  – Yes, he is.
③ Are you dancers?
  – No, I'm not.
④ Are the pencils yours?
  – No, they aren't.
⑤ Are you a singer?
  – No, I'm not.

MEMO

Grammar joy Answer

1

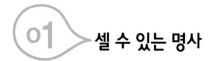

01 셀 수 있는 명사

① 1 cups   2 hats   3 houses   4 nurses
5 cities ▶city는 자음+y로 끝났으므로 y를 i로 고치고 es를 붙인다.
6 ladies   7 babies ▶baby는 자음+y로 끝났으므로 y를 i로 고치고 es를 붙인다.   8 countries   9 boys ▶boy는 모음+y로 끝났으므로 그냥 s만 붙여 복수형을 만든다.   10 toys   11 knives ▶fe로 끝났으므로 fe를 v로 고치고 es를 붙인다.   12 leaves ▶f로 끝났으므로 f를 v로 고치고 es를 붙인다.   13 wives   14 wolves
15 chefs ▶chef는 f로 끝나지만 f가 ves로 바뀌지 않고 s를 붙여 복수형을 만든다.   16 chiefs   17 scarf(e)s   18 roofs
19 potatoes ▶potato는 o로 끝나므로 es를 붙여 복수형을 만든다.
20 tomatoes   21 buses   22 boxes   23 dresses
24 dishes   25 memos   26 photos   27 videos
28 pianos ▶piano는 o로 끝나지만 es를 붙여 복수형으로 만들지 않고 s를 붙여 복수형을 만든다.   29 cellos   30 zoos

② 1 E   2 C   3 A   4 B   5 D   6 F

③ 1 maps   2 buses   3 boxes   4 boys
5 watches   6 knives   7 cities   8 cellos
9 brothers   10 memos   11 leaves   12 scarves, scarfs 13 dishes   14 potatoes   15 glasses

④ 1 videos   2 candies   3 wolves   4 nurses
5 pianos   6 photos   7 desks   8 churches
9 wives   10 monkeys   11 chefs   12 lions
13 countries   14 roofs ▶roof는 f로 끝났지만 s만 붙여서 복수형을 만드는 예외의 경우이다.   15 zoos

⑤ 1 leaves   2 chiefs   3 dresses ▶dress는 s로 끝났으므로 es를 붙인다.   4 erasers   5 potatoes
6 cell phones   7 ladies   8 knives   9 chefs
10 pictures   11 butterflies   12 trays ▶tray는 y로 끝났지만 모음+y로 끝났으므로 s만 붙인다.   13 beds   14 dishes
15 glasses ▶glass는 s로 끝났으므로 es를 붙인다.

⑥ 1 brushes   2 toys   3 lilies   4 tomatoes
5 dishes   6 students   7 scarves, scarfs   8 chairs
9 zoos 10 kids   11 churches   12 foxes ▶fox는 x로 끝났으므로 es를 붙인다.   13 classes ▶class는 s로 끝났으므로 es를 붙인다.   14 wives   15 countries ▶country는 자음+y로 끝났으므로 y를 i로 바꾸고 es를 붙인다.

⑦ 1 vases   2 dogs   3 cities   4 videos
5 knives   6 buses   7 memos   8 spoons
9 foxes   10 potatoes   11 windows
12 countries   13 zoos   14 roofs   15 dishes

⑧ 1 roommates   2 watches 3. knives
4 boxes   5 nurses ▶nurse는 e로 끝나므로 s만 붙여 복수형을 만든다.   6 pianos   7 photos   8 chiefs   9 babies
10 thieves ▶thief는 f로 끝나므로 f를 v로 바꾸고 es를 붙인다.
11 ladies ▶lady는 자음+y로 끝났으므로 y를 i로 고치고 es를 붙인다.   12 rulers   13 chefs   14 dresses   15 cellos

① 1 feet   2 teeth   3 geese   4 men
5 women   6 sportsmen   7 salesmen
8 policemen   9 fishermen   10 gentlemen
11 mailmen   12 oxen   13 children   14 mice
15 fish   16 deer ▶deer는 단수형과 복수형이 같다.
17 sheep   ▶fish, deer, sheep는 단수형과 복수형이 같다.
18 Japanese   19 Chinese   20 people

② 1 C   2 F   3 B   4 D   5 E   6 A

③ 1 fish   2 children   3 men   4 sheep
5 people   6 oxen   7 gentlemen   8 Chinese
9 Englishmen   10 deer   11 feet   12 teeth
13 mice   14 Japanese   15 geese

④ 1 women 2 sheep 3 policemen 4 deer
5 teeth 6 Chinese 7 children 8 fish 9 people
10 postmen 11 feet 12 geese 13 mice
14 oxen 15 fish

⑤ 1 sheep 2 men 3 mice 4 Japanese
5 people 6 oxen 7 geese 8 fish 9 mailmen
10 Chinese 11 feet 12 teeth 13 children
14 sportsmen 15 deer

⑥ 1 postmen 2 fish 3 policemen 4 deer
5 teeth 6 Chinese 7 women 8 children
9 oxen 10 sheep 11 feet 12 geese
13 people 14 mice 15 Japanese

실력 다지기
p.28~29

① 1 scarfs, scarves 2 feet 3 knives 4 fish
5 potatoes 6 zoos 7 toys 8 children
9 nurses 10 toothbrushes ▶toothbrush는 sh로 끝났으므
로 es를 붙인다. 11 dragonflies 12 mice 13 chiefs
14 pianos 15 postmen

② 1 geese 2 Japanese 3 ladies 4 oxen
5 wolves 6 deer 7 tomatoes 8 glasses
9 women 10 countries 11 houses 12 people
13 sheep 14 watches 15 foxes

실전Test
p.30~33

```
01 ④   02 ②   03 ⑤   04 ②   05 ④   06 ②
07 foxes, lions, deer   08 ②   09 ①   10 ③
```

01 child의 복수형은 children이다.

02 piano, radio, zoo, cello 등은 o로 끝나지만 es를 붙이지 않고 s만
을 붙이는 예외명사이다.

03 자음+y로 끝나는 명사는 y를 i로 고치고 es를 붙여 복수형을 만들고
(① lilies ② parties ③ butterflies ④ comedies), 모음+y로 끝나
는 명사의 복수형은 s만 붙인다.

04 classmates는 es를 붙여 복수형을 만든 것이 아니고, s를 붙여 복수
형을 만든 것이므로 단수형은 classmate이다.

05 roof는 f로 끝났지만 f를 v로 바꾸고 es를 붙이지 않고, 그대로 s만
붙여서 복수형을 만드는 예외의 경우이다.

06 one은 하나이므로 뒤에 단수형 명사가 오고, six와 two 다음에는 복
수형 명사가 온다.

08 church-churches/door-doors/ox-oxen

09 one은 '하나의'의 의미이므로 단수형인 brother가 와야 한다.

10 people은 그 자체가 복수이다.

 p.34

1 tree 2 geese 3 sheep 4 chefs 5 monkeys
6 mouse 7 oxen 8 lily 9 eyes 10 photos
11 postmen 12 deer 13 Chinese 14 leaf
15 boxes

02 셀 수 없는 명사

p.38~43

1 1 bread 4 music 5 food 7 money
9 oil 10 rice 12 butter 14 snow
15 shampoo

2 2 chocolate 4 cheese 5 gold 6 pepper
7 paper 8 sugar 11 furniture ▶furniture는 셀 수 없는
명사이므로 s가 붙지 않는다. 14 soap

3 1 cups, water 2 loaf, bread 3 bunches,
bananas ▶banana가 여러 개 달린 한 묶음이므로 복수형인 bananas
가 된다. bunch의 복수형은 ch로 끝났으므로 es를 붙여 bunches가 된다.
4 bags, rice 5 bottles, shampoo 6 carton,
milk 7 tubes, toothpaste 8 glasses, juice
9 pieces, furniture ▶furniture는 셀 수 없는 명사이므로 s를 붙
일 수 없다. 10 pieces, pizza 11 pieces, bread
12 bunches, grapes ▶grape는 포도가 한알씩 여러 개가 달려
한 송이가 되므로 복수형인 grapes가 된다. 13 bars, soap
14 sheet, paper 15 jars, pickles

4 1 jars 2 cans 3 jars 4 piece 5 piece
6 cartons 7 pieces 8 bars 9 bags 10 piece
11 pieces 12 bottles 13 cartons 14 loaves ▶
a loaf of bread는 빵 한 덩어리, a piece of bread는 빵 한 조각이다.
loaf의 복수형은 loaves이다. 15 piece

5 1 pieces 2 pieces 3 glasses 4 pieces
5 cans 6 bunches, bananas 7 glasses
8 pieces 9 bottles 10 tubes 11 bags
12 sheets 13 piece 14 bars 15 cartons

6 1 cans 2 pieces 3 jars 4 glasses
5 bunches 6 bars 7 cups 8 cans,corn
9 pieces, furniture 10 cartons 11 pieces
12 bags 13 pieces 14 bottles 15 loaves ▶하나
이상이므로 계량 단위를 단수(loaf)가 아닌 복수 loaves로 나타낸다.

p.44~45

1 1 bunches 2 cans 3 bars 4 carton
5 pieces 6 loaves 7 pieces 8 cups 9 bags
10 cans 11 tubes 12 bunches 13 cartons
14 pieces 15 pieces

2 1 cartons 2 bottles 3 bars 4 sheets
(pieces) 5 bottles 6 pieces(slices) 7 pieces
8 bags 9 cups 10 jars 11 pieces 12 pieces
13 bottles 14 cans 15 pieces

p.46~47

1 1 teas → tea 2 pickle → pickles ▶pickle은 한 병
에 여러 개 담겨 있으므로 pickles가 된다. 3 loaf → loaves
4 cans → can 5 banana → bananas 6 glass →
glasses 7 shampoos → shampoo 8 bottle →
bottles 9 loaves → pieces(slices) 10 bunches →
pieces 11 musics → music 12 grape → grapes
13 jar → bars 14 rices → rice 15 papers → paper

2 1 bunches → jars 2 glass → glasses 3 cans
→ bottles 4 piece → pieces 5 cheeses → cheese
6 bunch → bunches 7 piece → bag 8 tubes →
jars 9 cans → can 10 bars → tubes 11 slices →
sheets(pieces) 12 informations → information
13 cartons → bunches 14 pieces → piece
15 tube → bar

01 ③　02 ①　03 ③　04 ①　05 ⑤
06 loaves　07 bar, tubes, bunches　08 ⑤
09 ③ - ② - ①　10 piece → pieces

02 셀 수 없는 명사(soup, oil, water, sugar)에는 s를 붙여 복수형을
만들 수 없다.

03 ③ a bunch of → a piece of

04 여섯 개의 can이므로 cans이다.

05 rice의 계량 단위는 bag이다.

06 덩어리의 빵은 loaf로 표현하며, loaf의 복수형은 loaves이다.

08 hair는 셀 수 없는 명사이므로 s를 붙여 복수형을 만들 수 없다.
hairs → hair

10 two는 복수를 나타내므로 piece의 복수형인 pieces가 되어야 한다.

p.52

1 glasses　2 piece　3 pieces, sheets　4 loaves
5 bags　6 bar　7 piece　8 bottle　9 cans
10 bunches　11 cartons　12 tubes　13 jars
14 bunches　15 piece

○3 관사

① 1 a　2 ×　3 ×　4 × ▶소유격이 올 때는 관사를 붙이지
않는다. 5 an　6 × ▶houses가 복수형이므로 관사가 필요 없
다.
7 a　8 ×　9 ×　10 a　11 ×　12 a　13 a　14 ×
15 a

② 1 ×　2 an ▶honest의 h가 묵음이므로 a대신 an을 붙인다.
3 ×　4 ×　5 a　6 ×　7 a　8 × ▶tomatoes가 복수형이므
로 관사가 필요없다. 9 ×　10 ×　11 a　12 ×　13 a
14 ×　15 ×

③ 1 a　2 an　3 ×　4 ×　5 an　6 ×　7 ×　8 a
9 a　10 a　11 ×　12 ×　13 ×　14 an　15 a　16 ×
17 ×　18 ×　19 ×　20 ×　21 an　22 ×　23 ×
24 a　25 ×　26 ×　27 ×　28 ×　29 ×　30 an

④ 1 ×　2 ×　3 ×　4 ×　5 ×　6 an　7 ×　8 ×
9 × ▶America는 모음으로 시작하지만 고유명사이므로 관사(an)를 붙
이지 않는다. 10 ×　11 a ▶university는 모음 글자인 u로 시작
하지만 발음이 자음으로 나기 때문에 a를 붙인다. 12 a　13 ×
14 ×　15 a　16 a　17 an　18 an　19 a　20 ×
21 an　22 ×　23 ×　24 ×　25 ×　26 ×　27 ×
28 ×　29 an　30 a

⑤ 1 ×　2 the　3 the　4 the　5 the　6 the
7 the　8 ×　9 the　10 × ▶운동 이름 앞에는 the를 붙이지
않는다. 11 the ▶강, 바다 이름 앞에는 the를 붙인다. 12 the
13 the　14 ×　15 the ▶호텔, 식당, 극장, 박물관 앞에는
the를 붙인다.

6 **1** the **2** the **3** × **4** × ▶식사 이름 앞에는 the를 붙이지 않는다. **5** the **6** the **7** the **8** the **9** × **10** × **11** the **12** the ▶강 이름 앞에는 the를 붙인다. **13** the ▶'the +먹(고)+자(고)+구(경)+악(기)'에 따라 인공물 중에서 hotel은 자는 곳이므로 the를 붙여준다. **14** × **15** ×

1 **1** × ▶milk는 셀 수 없는 명사이기 때문에 a, an이 필요 없다. **2** a **3** an **4** the ▶박물관은 인공물 중에 구경하는 곳에 해당하므로 the를 붙인다. **5** a **6** × **7** × ▶sugar는 셀 수 없는 명사이므로 관사를 붙일 수 없다. **8** ×, The **9** × **10** × **11** an **12** × **13** × **14** an **15** An ▶hour는 자음글자인 h로 시작하지만 h가 묵음이므로 앞에 an을 붙인다.

2 **1** a **2** ×, The **3** an **4** × ▶거리, 공항, 역, 대학 이름 앞에는 the를 붙이지 않는다. **5** × **6** × **7** a **8** × **9** × **10** a **11** a **12** an, The **13** ×, an **14** the **15** the ▶식당은 인공물 중에 먹는 곳에 해당하므로 the를 붙인다.

3 **1** a **2** an **3** a **4** The **5** × **6** The **7** ▶공항 이름앞에는 관사를 붙이지 않는다. **8** ×, × **9** A, The **10** × **11** × **12** a **13** ×, × **14** × **15** ×, an ▶honest는 자음글자인 h로 시작하지만 h가 묵음이므로 앞에 an을 붙인다.

4 **1** the **2** × **3** a, The **4** the **5** × **6** The **7** The, the **8** The, the ▶세상에 하나밖에 없는 자연물 앞에는 the를 붙인다. **9** × **10** × **11** an, The **12** The **13** the **14** × **15** the

1 **1** barbers → barber **2** a → × ▶Japan은 고유명사이므로 a를 붙이지 않는다. **3** a → an **4** a → × **5** an → a ▶모음으로 시작하지만 발음이 [j], [w]인 경우 a를 붙인다. **6** a → × ▶large는 형용사이므로 a를 붙이지 않는다. **7** A → The ▶이미 정해진 것을 나타낼 때는 정관사 the를 쓴다. **8** a → × **9** an → a ▶모음으로 시작하지만 발음이 [j], [w]인 경우 a를 붙인다. **10** a → × **11** pumpkin → pumpkins **12** A → The ▶앞에 나온 명사 cheese를 다시 언급하므로 the를 붙인다. **13** a → an **14** a → an **15** oxen → ox ▶단수인 ox로 고쳐야 한다.

2 **1** the → × **2** middle → the middle **3** right → the right **4** the → × **5** The Kennedy airport → Kennedy airport ▶공항 앞에는 the를 붙이지 않는다. **6** the Seoul Station → Seoul Station **7** end → the end **8** A → The **9** the → × ▶습관적으로 listen to music로 쓴다. **10** An → The ▶세상에 하나 밖에 없는 자연물 앞에는 the를 붙인다. **11** top → the top **12** A → The **13** the → × **14** Shilla Hotel → The Shilla Hotel **15** a → an

실전Test

01 ① 02 ④ 03 ②, ⑤ 04 ④ 05 ②, ③ 06 ② 07 ③ 08 ③ 09 ③ 10 A sugar → Sugar

01 ① an eggplant ② a mailbox ③ a tulip ④ a computer ⑤ a dragonfly

02 honest는 h가 묵음이므로 관사로 an을 취한다.

03 ② 소유격 앞에는 a(an)을 붙이지 않는다. ⑤ 세상에 하나밖에 없는 자연물 앞에는 the를 붙인다.

04 ① 식사 이름 앞에는 관사를 붙이지 않는다. ② 운동 종목 앞에는 관사를 붙이지 않는다. ③ 고유명사 앞에는 관사를 붙이지 않는다. ④ 악기 앞에는 the를 붙인다. ⑤ 공항 이름 앞에는 관사를 붙이지 않는다.

05 ② 주어가 복수이므로 a를 붙이지 않고 singers가 되어야 한다. ③ 주어인 they가 복수이고 women이 복수형이므로 a를 붙이지 않는다.

6 **Grammar Joy 1**

06 hour는 자음으로 시작하지만 h가 묵음이므로 an을 붙인다.

07 정해지지 않은 명사 앞에는 부정관사 a,an을, 이미 정해진 명사 앞에는 정관사 the를 사용한다.

08 ①고유명사 앞에는 a(an)을 붙이지 않는다. ② 모음으로 시작하는 형용사와 함께 쓰인 명사 앞에는 an을 붙인다. ④ 명사가 없고 형용사만 있을 때는 a(an)을 붙이지 않는다. ⑤ 식사 이름 앞에는 관사를 붙이지 않는다.

09 위치를 나타내는 말 앞에는 the를 붙인다. the left, the right, the top, the end, the middle

10 sugar는 셀 수 없는 명사이므로 a가 올 수 없다.

 **p.72**

1 × 2 the 3 × 4 an 5 × 6 the 7 The, the
8 The 9 the 10 × 11 the 12 an, The 13 ×
14 the 15 the

 인칭대명사와 지시대명사

기초다지기 p.76~81

① 1 you 2 they 3 we 4 those 5 they
6 these 7 they

1 this 2 you 3 he 4 it 5 I 6 that 7 she

② 1 3, 복수 2 3, 단수 ▶my(나의)가 있지만 초점은 hand이므로 3인칭 단수이다. 3 1, 단수 4 3, 복수 5 3, 단수
6 3, 단수 ▶your(너희)가 있지만 초점은 face이므로 3인칭 단수이다.
7 1, 복수 8 2, 복수 9 3, 복수 10 3, 복수
11 3, 단수 12 3, 복수 13 3, 단수 14 3, 복수 ▶my(나의)가 있지만 초점은 sisters이므로 3인칭 복수이다. 15 2, 단수

③ 1 3, 단수 2 1, 단수 3 3, 복수 4 3, 복수
5 1, 복수 6 3, 단수 7 3, 복수 ▶my(나의)가 있지만 초점은 hats이므로 3인칭 복수이다. 8 3, 단수 ▶your(너의)가 있지만 초점은 grandmother이므로 3인칭 단수이다. 9 2, 복수 10 3, 복수
11 3, 단수 12 3, 단수 13 3, 복수 ▶our(우리의)가 있지만 초점은 classes이므로 3인칭 복수이다. 14 2, 단수 15 3, 복수

④ 1 I 2 This 3 Those ▶Tom's shirts가 복수 이므로 주어도 복수가 되어야 한다. 4 You ▶parents가 복수이므로 주어도 복수가 되어야 하며 you는 단수와 복수가 같다. 5 It 6 They
7 This 8 They 9 That 10 We 11 You
12 These 13 Tom 14 Tom and Judy 15 That

⑤ 1 These 2 I 3 They ▶children은 child의 복수이다.
4 It 5 John and Tom 6 We 7 This 8 Those
9 The men 10 She 11 It 12 You 13 They
▶mice는 mouse의 복수형이다. 14 Seoul and Busan
15 She

6 1 a fly 2 flies 3 a shopkeeper 4 a farmer
5 her cousins 6 my sunflowers 7 He 8 juice
9 soldiers 10 a blue diamond 11 melons
12 his daughters 13 bread 14 a ticket
15 my notebooks

꼭꼭다지기   p.82~85

1 1 This 2 They 3 Those 4 This 5 We
6 You 7 That 8 They 9 Those 10 She
11 This 12 These 13 You 14 They 15 It

2 1 They 2 This 3 Those 4 He 5 It
6 These 7 It 8 We 9 These 10 You 11 He
12 Those 13 They 14 They 15 They

3 1 They 2 These 3 He 4 Those 5 We
6 This 7 They 8 You 9 It 10 Those 11 These
12 That 13 These 14 She 15 They

4 1 coaches 2 engineer 3 trains 4 coins
5 cars 6 wolf 7 bull 8 daughter 9 tigers
10 photographers 11 box 12 potatoes
13 scientists 14 postmen 15 sisters

실력다지기   p.86~87

1 1 violinist → violinists ▶주어가 복수이므로 보어도 복
수 2 vests → vest 3 girl → girls 4 canes → cane
5 doctor → doctors 6 rose → roses 7 tennis
players → tennis player 8 They → It 9 wives →
wife 10 men → man 11 These → This
12 artists → artist 13 dogs → dog 14 kiwi →
kiwis 15 They → She

1 1 women → woman 2 guys → guy
3 movie → movies 4 nieces → niece 5 kings →
king 6 ring → rings 7 boys → boy 8 girls → girl
▶Ann은 단수이므로 단수인 girl이 보어로 와야 한다. 9 It → They
10 teacher → teachers 11 Those → That
12 fisherman → fishermen ▶Jim and Tom은 복수이므로 보
어도 복수인 fishermen이 되어야 한다. 13 animal → animals
14 ladies → lady 15 gentlemen → gentleman
▶주어인 boss가 단수이므로 보어도 단수형인 gentleman이 되어야 한다.

실전Test   p.88~91

| 01 ⑤ | 02 ③ | 03 ⑤ | 04 we, I | 05 ⑤ |
| 06 ② | 07 ① | 08 ② | 09 ③ | 10 ③ |

03 보어인 painter가 단수이므로 주어도 단수가 와야만 한다.

04 I는 1인칭 단수, we는 1인칭 복수

05 주어진 문장에서 주어인 he가 단수이므로 boys는 단수형인 boy가
되어야 한다.

06 주어가 단수이면 보어도 단수이어야 한다.

07 this의 복수형은 these이고, that의 복수형은 those이다.

08 ①, ③, ④, ⑤는 사람을 가리키고, ②는 사물을 가리킨다.

09 주어 those가 복수이므로 보어도 복수형이 와야 한다.

10 ①, ②, ④, ⑤는 보어가 단수이므로 'you'가 단수이고 ③은 보어가
복수이므로 'you'가 복수이다. you는 단수와 복수가 같으므로 유의
하도록 한다.

 p.92

1 We 2 They 3 You 4 children 5 Those
6 aunt 7 I 8 cars 9 You 10 house
11 These 12 They 13 farmers 14 He 15 You

Unit 1-Unit 2

01

1 a, e, i, o, u

02

1 셀 수 있는 명사 : 2, 3, 6, 7, 10

  셀 수 없는 명사 : 1, 4, 5, 8, 9

03

1 boxes   2 knives   3 pianos   4 deer   5 candies

6 watches   7 chairs   8 buses   9 women

10 feet

04

1 dresses   2 fish   3 cities   4 rooms   5 churches

6 potatoes   7 mice   8 erasers   9 foxes

10 tomatoes   11 flies   12 dishes   13 zoos

14 children   15 teeth

Unit 3

01

1 cans   2 piece   3 loaves   4 glasses   5 bunches

6 jars   7 cups   8 bags   9 slices   10 cartons

11 sheets, paper   12 pieces, furniture

13 cans, corn ▶corn은 rice처럼 한알 한알 헤아리기가 힘들기 때문에 셀 수 없는 명사로 취급한다.   14 bottles   15 bars

02

1 bunches   2 jars   3 cartons   4 bags

5 cans   6 bottles   7 pieces   8 glasses   9 bars

10 piece   11 tubes   12 bunches   13 bottles

14 pieces(sheets)   15 piece

Unit 4

01

1 ×   2 The   3 an   4 ×   5 ×   6 the   7 ×

8 A, The   9 the   10 the   11 ×   12 an   13 a

14 ×   15 the

02

1 a   2 The, the   3 ×   4 ×   5 a   6 a, The   7 ×

8 ×   9 the   10 ×   11 the   12 the   13 The

14 the   15 ×

---

01 ③   02 o, l, a, eau, i, u, ou, ai   03 ③, ④

04 ②   05 ②   06 knife → knives   07 ①

08 ④   09 ②, ③   10 ①, ②   11 ②   12 the breakfast → breakfast   13 ⑤   14 ③   15 ②

16 ①   17 ⑤   18 The   19 ⑤   20 ②, ⑤

21 ②, ⑤   22 ④   23 rooms, wolves, foxes

24 an, a   25 ⑤

03 ① baby-babies ③ dish-dishes ④ ball-balls ⑤ leaf-leaves

06 knife-knives

07 ① candy-candies

09 a,e,i,o,u로 시작하는 명사 앞에는 an을 붙인다.

11 the lunch-lunch 식사 앞에는 the를 붙이지 않는다.

13 정해진 명사 앞에는 the를 붙인다.

14 셀 수 없는 명사 앞에는 a(an)을 붙일 수 없으나 the는 가능하다.

16 사람이름 앞에 , 셀 수 없는 명사 앞에, 나라 이름 앞에, 복수명사 앞에는 a를 붙일 수 없다.

17 연주하는 악기 앞에는 the를 붙인다.

19 보어 guys가 복수이므로 주어는 복수가 와야 한다.

05 지시대명사와 지시형용사

p.108~111

1
1 지시대명사 2 지시형용사 3 지시형용사 4 지시대명사
5 지시형용사 6 지시대명사 7 지시대명사 8 지시대명사
9 지시형용사 10 지시대명사 11 지시대명사 12 지시형용사
13 지시대명사 14 지시형용사 15 지시형용사

2
1 dogs, dog, rice
2 pictures, picture, chocolate
3 dress, dresses, Coke

1 that, those, that
2 these, this, this
3 soap, pots, pot

3 1 they 2 we ▶I가 포함되면 we로 받는다. 3 you
▶you가 포함되면 you로 받는다. 4 she 5 you 6 we
7 it 8 they 9 they 10 you 11 it 12 they
13 they ▶uncles가 복수이므로 they로 받는다. 14 he ▶uncle
이 남자이므로 he로 받는다. 15 they

4 1 it 2 we 3 he 4 she 5 they 6 they
7 they 8 you 9 we 10 he 11 they 12 it
13 it 14 you 15 they

p.112~117

1
1 those buses　　　　2 these boys
3 those sheep　　　　4 those sweaters
5 the vests　　　　　6 these letters
7 those trains　　　　8 these pencils

9 those barbers　　　10 the sofas
11 those fish　　　　12 those men
13 these lilies　　　　14 the teeth
15 these leaves

2 1 those rings 2 these oxen 3 the men
4 the babies 5 those mice 6 the photos
7 these videos 8 those carrots 9 those chiefs
10 the elephants 11 these ladies 12 those kids
13 those ships 14 these jumpers
15 the women

3 1 those ants 2 these zoos 3 the benches
4 those snakes 5 these bugs 6 the hot dogs
7 these memos 8 those mice 9 those feet
10 these pianos 11 those cities 12 these trucks
13 the glasses 14 those sportsmen
15. these deer

4 1 those cities 2 the models 3 these taxis
4 these cellos 5 the children 6 those dishes
7 those melons 8 the flowers 9 those sweet
potatoes 10 these trains 11 those farmers
12 these knives 13 the babies 14 those violins
15 the cookies

5 1 these books 2 that desk 3 the pots
4 the juice 5 those oxen 6 this coat 7 these
computers 8 those toys 9 the gloves
10 this student 11 that bread 12 the doll
13 these candies 14 the churches
15 this paper

6 1 this water 2 the boats 3 that store
4 the tomatoes 5 those tigers 6 this picture
7 the scarfs(scarves) 8 that cheese 9 this oil
10 the cook 11 that fan 12 the butter 13
those socks 14 these doctors 15 those buses

 **p.118~119**

1 1 star → stars 2 they → the 3 this → these
4 tulip → tulips 5 that → those 6 deers → deer
7 videoes → videos 8 strawberry → strawberries
9 map → maps 10 this → these 11 sheeps →
sheep 12 they → the 13 lamp → lamps
14 this → these 15 postman → postmen

2 1 they 2 we 3 she 4 you 5 it 6 he
7 they 8 they 9 we 10 they 11 she 12 he
13 they 14 they 15 you

실전Test **p.120~123**

> 01 ③ 02 ⑤ 03 ① 04 ⑤ 05 ⑤
> 06 ④ 07 ⑤ 08 The cucumber 09 That
> school bag 10 They

01 ①, ②, ④, ⑤는 지시대명사이고, ③은 지시형용사이다.

02 your mouth → it, Mr.Han and Mrs.Han → they, John and you → you, my brothers → they

03 ① she and I → we

04 ⑤ that memo → those memos

05 Tommy, Joe가 you와 함께 있으므로 복수인 you(너희들)가 된다.

08 The cucumbers의 단수형은 The cucumber이다.

09 단수 지시형용사 뒤에 오는 명사도 단수형이 와야 하므로 those schoolbags의 단수형인 that schoolbag이 와야 한다.

10 Mr. Kim and Mrs. Kim은 3인칭 복수이므로 대명사 they로 받아 준다.

Quiz! **p.124**

1 it 2 she 3 it 4 you 5 we 6 they 7 it
8 they

1 wolves 2 box 3 nurse 4 soap 5 roofs
6 oranges 7 those 8 girls

 06 **인칭대명사의 격변화**

기초다지기 **p.128~135**

1
my, me, yours, he, his, 그를(에게), his, 그녀. 그녀의,
her, hers, its, it

we, 우리들의, us, ours, 너희들은, your, 너희들을(에게),
yours, their, them, 그들의 것

누가, whose, whom, 누구의 것

Tom's, Tom을(에게), Tom's

my sister's, my sister, 나의 여동생의 것

2 1 는 2 의 것 3 을. 에게 4 의 것 5 를. 에게 6 의
7 의 8 의 9 을. 에게 10 을. 에게 11 는 12 의
13 을. 에게 14 를.에게 15 은 16 를. 에게 17 의 것
18 를. 에게 19 은 20 의 21 의 것 22 를. 에게
23 의 것 24 의 25 은 26 는 27 은 28 의 것
29 의 것 30 은

3 1 me 2 his 3 him 4 them 5 you 6 my
sister's 7 our 8 whose 9 Tom 10 us
11 her 12 Tom's 13 it 14 his 15 them
16 her 17 mine 18 their 19 we 20 my
21 whom 22 you 23 theirs 24 their 25 my
sister 26 he 27 you 28 hers 29 Tom's 30 it

4 1 her 2 Tom's 3 me 4 who 5 theirs
6 yours 7 you 8 him 9 it 10 my sister
11 yours 12 whom 13 we 14 she 15 his
16 Tom's 17 your 18 them 19 Tom 20 ours
21 whose 22 its 23 mine 24 us 25 your
26 my sister's 27 their 28 whose 29 my
30 their

5 1 your 2 whose 3 them 4 his 5 they
6 their 7 her 8 me 9 my 10 hers 11 whom
12 them 13 her 14 Tom 15 him 16 ours
17 my sister's 18 her 19 mine 20 Tom's
21 us 22 whose 23 its 24 our 25 his
26 you 27 their 28 yours 29 you 30 my
sister's

6 1 whose 2 you 3 their 4 hers 5 us
6 its 7 his 8 Tom 9 mine 10 whose
11 them 12 yours 13 your 14 my sister
15 Tom's 16 he 17 her 18 your 19 we
20 whom 21 his 22 my sister's 23 her
24 theirs 25 ours 26 you 27 yours
28 Tom's 29 our 30 him

7 1 my 2 Judy's 3 It 4 the boy's 5 his
6 We 7 them 8 me 9 theirs 10 yours
11 her 12 hers 13 our 14 You, it 15 She

8 1 their 2 me 3 Tom 4 ours 5 hers
6 They, his 7 our 8 Her 9 You, my 10 mine
11 She, us 12 theirs 13 his 14 your 15 My
sister's

꼭꼭 다지기   p.136~141

1 1 We 2 your 3 him 4 us 5 you
6 Their 7 Jane's 8 yours 9 him 10 my father's
11 her 12 I, her 13 her 14 ours 15 the boy

2 1 me 2 Mr. Kim, his 3 us 4 theirs
5 She, him 6 hers 7 us 8 He, me 9 them
10 her 11 Jane 12 Its 13 His 14 hers
15 She, you

3 1 my 2 She 3 theirs 4 him 5 her 6 it
7 your 8 her 9 ours 10 Ann 11 his
12 their 13 hers 14 my 15 him

4 1 the man's 2 us 3 Sumi's 4 Its
5 them 6 her 7 Sujin's 8 her 9 mine
10 They, her 11 His 12 us 13 the farmer's
14 my 15 ours

5 1 us 2 Her 3 He 4 him 5 ours 6 The
boy's 7 James 8 him 9 Her 10 his 11 Our
12 Insu's 13 mine 14 You 15 She, you

6 1 them 2 My 3 her 4 Mary's 5 yours
6 me 7 our 8 them 9 Jane's 10 us
11 theirs 12 Your 13 it 14 He 15 Their

실력 다지기   p.142~143

1 1 him → his 2 my → mine 3 she → her
4 their → them 5 we → us 6 We → Our 7 I → my
8 hers → her 9 mine → my 10 they → their
11 My → I 12 Jennys → Jenny's 13 the farmer →
the farmer's 14 his → him 15 Her → She

2 1 Tom's → Tom 2 them → their 3 I → me
4 her → hers 5 he → his 6 my sister's → my sister
7 We → Our 8 hers → her 9 their → theirs
10 It → Its 11 your → you 12 you → yours
13 Their → They 14 Tom → Tom's 15 Its → It

01 ③   02 ④   03 ①   04 ⑤   05 ③
06 ①   07 ②   08 ③   09 ⑤   10 ④

02 they의 소유대명사는 theirs이다.

03 '이 그림은 그녀의 것이다'라는 의미의 문장이므로 '그녀의 것'에 해
   당하는 hers가 와야 옳다.

04 we는 주격, we의 소유격은 our, 목적격은 us이다.

05 주격이 올 수 있는 자리이다.

06 전치사 뒤에는 목적격이 온다.

07 '그것의 색깔'이므로 it의 소유격 Its가 온다.

08 목적격이 와야 하므로 him과 her가 옳다.

09 ⑤는 목적격이 아니라 주격이다.

10 your dresses는 소유대명사 yours로 바꿔 쓸 수 있다. her father는
   목적격 him으로 바꿔 쓸 수 있다.

p.148

1 me   2 ours   3 My friend's   4 him   5 her
6 them   7 her   8 His   9 Mr. William's   10 your
11 mine   12 ours   13 us   14 your   15 her

07 be동사의 긍정문

기초다지기   p.152~157

① 1 am   2 are   3 is   4 is   5 are   6 is   7 are
8 are   9 are ▶Tom and Jim은 복수이므로 are을 사용한다.
10 is   11 are   12 is ▶The game은 단수이므로 is가 온다.
13 are ▶The games는 복수이므로 are이 온다.   14 are   15 is

② 1 is   2 is   3 are   4 are   5 is   6 are   7 is
8 is   9 am   10 are   11 are   12 are   13 is   14 is
▶policeman은 단수이므로 is가 온다.   15 are ▶policemen은 복수
이므로 are이 온다.

③ 1 are   2 is   3 is   4 are   5 are   6 is   7 are
8 is   9 are   10 is   11 are   12 are   13 are
14 is   15 am

④ 1 are   2 is   3 are   4 is   5 are   6 is   7 are
8 are   9 is   10 are   11 are   12 is   13 are
14 are   15 is

⑤ 1 These watches are ▶주어와 be동사 모두 복수형으로
만든다.   2 Those kites are   3 The ladies are
4 The shoe stores are   5 We are ▶I는 1인칭 단수, we는
1인칭 복수이다.   6 The churches are   7 You are
8 Those tomatoes are   9 The women are
10 These goats are

⑥ 1 are nurses   2 are scientists   3 are fresh
4 are my daughters   5 are yours   6 are painters
7 are children   8 are wolves   9 are great
10 are mice

1

1 These are
2 These lights are
3 The candies are
4 You are
5 Those benches are
6 We are
7 They are
8 The postmen are
9 Those tables are
10 These doors are

2

1 are oranges
2 are models
3 are policemen
4 are his
5 are busy
6 are erasers
7 are dancers
8 are diligent
9 are hers
10 are cute

3

1 They are presidents
2 These are fish
3 They are cashiers
4 Those dresses are wonderful
5 The sportsmen are healthy
6 These are lions
7 We are dentists
8 The flies are dirty
9 These black cars are mine
10 They are smart monkeys

4

1 They are textbooks
2 These are geese
3 Those ladies are beautiful
4 We are artists
5 These knives are sharp
6 You are writers
7 Those cows are hers
8 These are Jane's skirts
9 The rooms are messy
10 They are old hairdressers

5

1 is tired.
2 is his
3 are housekeepers
4 is an insect
5 are fallen leaves
6 is sweet
7 are my new friends
8 is a barber
9 are gentlemen
10 is a very shining star

6

1 is a bear
2 are my bodyguards
3 is yours
4 are free
5 are my nephews
6 is a monster
7 is a carpenter
8 is yellow
9 are very heavy stones
10 are clever boys

1 1 are → is 2 is → are 3 engineer → engineers 4 towel → towels 5 lazys → lazy 6 soldiers → a soldier 7 am → is 8 is → are 9 honests → honest 10 The men → The man 11 is → are 12 is → are 13 mines → mine 14 are → is 15 carpenter → carpenters

2 1 are → is 2 postmen → postman 3 flower → flowers 4 are → is 5 is → are 6 is → are 7 chickens → chicken 8 mouse → mice 9 is → are 10 is → are 11 am → are 12 peach → peaches 13 rings → ring 14 are → is 15 raincoat → raincoats

실전Test

p.166~169

01 ④ 02 ② 03 ③ 04 ② 05 ⑤
06 ① 07 ③ 08 ① 09 are 10 ⑤

01 we가 취하는 be동사는 are이다.

02 주어인 Those가 복수이므로 be동사는 are를 써야 한다.

03 ①, ②, ④, ⑤는 주어가 3인칭 단수이므로 is를 써야 하고, 주어가 복수인 ③은 are를 써야 한다.

04 주어가 모두 복수이므로 be동사는 are를 사용한다.

05 ① is → are ② are → am ③ is → are ④ is → are

07 Jane and I는 복수이므로 복수 be동사 are를 사용한다.

08 ②, ③, ④, ⑤의 'is'는 '~이다'의 의미이고, ①의 'is'는 '~있다'의 의미이다.

09 주어가 민수와 수빈, 복수이므로 be동사는 are를 사용한다.

10 be동사가 단수이므로 주어는 단수가 와야 한다.

p.170

1 is 2 is 3 are 4 are 5 are

1 These are strong oxen.
2 We are too late.
3 They are singers.
4 His shirts are colorful.
5 They are yellow umbrellas.

 be동사의 부정문, 의문문

 p.174~177

1 1 I'm 2 aren't 3 She's 4 isn't 5 You're
6 It's 7 That's 8 We're 9 They're 10 He's

2 1 I'm, not 2 She(She's), isn't(not)
3 They(They're), aren't(not) 4 He(He's), isn't(not)
5 We(We're), aren't(not) 6 You(You're), aren't(not)
7 That(That's), isn't(not) 8 It(It's), isn't(not)
9 She(She's), isn't(not) 10 You(You're), aren't(not)

3 1 Am, I 2 Are, you 3 Is, he 4 Is, Mary
5 Are, you 6 Is, the giraffe 7 Is, that 8 Is, she
9 Are, they 10 Are, these

4 1 Am, I 2 They(They're), aren't(not)
3 Is, it 4 We(We're), aren't(not) 5 Is, she
6 He(He's), isn't(not) 7 Is, his concert
8 The woman, isn't 9 Is, Jane's hair 10 This, isn't

 p.178~181

1
1 you are, you are
2 I'm not, we are
3 it is, they aren't ▶'this'로 물으면 'it'으로 대답하고 복수인 'these'로 물으면 'they'로 대답한다.
4 it is, they are ▶'that'으로 물으면 'it'으로 대답하고 복수인 'those'로 물으면 'they'로 대답한다.
5 I'm not, we are
6 it isn't, they are

②

1 he is, they are

2 it is, they are ▶the window는 3인칭 단수이므로 it로 받고, the windows는 3인칭 복수이므로 they로 받는다.

3 he is, they(they're) aren't(not)

4 it is, they(they're) aren't(not)

5 you(you're) aren't(not), you(we) are ▶대답하는 사람이 같은 일행이면 we로 받는다.

6 I'm not, we are

③ 1 it, yours 2 they are 3 she is, She, his
4 it is 5 they, yours 6 it is, your 7 they aren't
8 he, our 9 they're, They(They're) aren't(not) 10 they, your(our)

④ 1 they, ours 2 she(she's) isn't(not) 3 it, his
4 are 5 it, It, my 6 they are 7 isn't, isn't her
8 they, your 9 They, his 10 aren't your(our)
▶대답하는 사람이 같은 일행이면 our로 받는다.

p.182~183

① 1 this → it 2 are → am 3 she's → she is
▶'Yes, she is.'에서 축약형은 쓰지 않는다. 4 isn't → aren't
▶my husband and Tom은 복수이다. 5 you are → we are
▶질문속의 you가 복수이므로 we로 대답해야 한다. 6 is → are
7 we aren't → I'm not 8 is → isn't 9 is → are
10 he is → they are 11 isn't → aren't 12 is → are
13 I'm not → you aren't(you're not) 14 Are → Is
15 we're → I'm

② 1 these → they 2 I am → we are 3 is not →
is 4 it's → it is 5 not are → are not 6 we are →
we aren't(we're not) 7 not is → is not 8 he is →
they are 9 I am → you are 10 they're → they are
11 he is → they are 12 that → it 13 this → it
14 those → they 15 we aren't → I'm not

01 ② 02 ⑤ 03 ④ 04 Is your uncle
diligent?,Your uncle is not(isn't) diligent.
05 ③ 06 ⑤ 07 ④ 08 ③ 09 ③, ⑤ 10 ②

01 be동사의 부정문은 be동사 바로 뒤에 not을 붙인다.

02 you(단수)로 물어보면 I로 대답한다.

03 주어 the buildings가 복수이므로 대답은 they로 받는다.

04 be동사의 의문문은 be동사를 주어 바로 앞으로 보내어 만들고, be동사의 부정문은 be동사 바로 뒤에 not을 붙이면 된다.

06 복수형 you로 질문하면, we로 대답한다.

07 This is는 축약형을 만들 수 없다.

10 you로 물어보면 단수일 때는 I로, 복수일 때는 we로 대답한다.

Quiz! p.188

1 Are you hungry?

2 The boy isn't very kind.

3 Are they singers?

4 It isn't (It's not) his digital camera.

5 Are those erasers yours?

1 I am 2 they are 3 it isn't(it's not) 4 we are
5 he isn't(he's not)

Review Test 2 p.190~197

Unit 5

01
1 These 2 We 3 They 4 That 5 You 6 He
7 These

02
1 She 2 They 3 You 4 This 5 Those 6 We
7 It

03

1 the tigers 2 these hens 3 those beds
4 the babies 5 those children 6 the photos
7 these coats

04

1 those boys 2 these mice 3 the leaves
4 those houses 5 these hamburgers
6 the strawberries 7 those dishes

Unit 6

01

1 my, me, mine.   your, you, yours,
 his, him, his,   her, her, hers,
 its, it,   our, us, ours
 your, you, yours,   their, them, theirs
 whose, whom, whose

02

1 Tom's, Tom, Tom's
 my sister's, my sister, my sister's

03

1 her 2 mine 3 me 4 our 5 Tom's
6 my sister 7 his 8 yours 9 its 10 theirs
11 your 12 him 13 ours 14 hers

04

1 him 2 her 3 us 4 mine 5 them 6 Tom's
7 Its

Unit 7

01

1 is 2 is 3 are 4 are 5 is 6 is 7 are 8 is
9 Are 10 is 11 are 12 are 13 is 14 are
15 am

02

1 is 2 is 3 are 4 is 5 are 6 is 7 are 8 is
9 are 10 are 11 are 12 is 13 am 14 are
15 are

Unit 8

01

1 I'm not 2 Are they 3 Is it 4 We're not(We're

not) 5 She isn't (She's not) 6 Is Jane 7 Here
isn't (Here's not) 8 Is your sister 9 Those
paintings aren't 10 Are Tom and John

02

1 he is. 2 I'm not. 3 you are. 4 they aren't.
5 we aren't. 6 it is. 7 it isn't. 8 she is. 9 they
are. 10 they aren't.

내/신/대/비 2   p.198~202

01 ② 02 ③, ⑤ 03 ④ 04 ③ 05 ④, ⑤ 06 ④
07 ① 08 ③ 09 our 10 ① 11 ③ 12 ④
13 ④ 14 ② 15 ② 16 ④ 17 They aren't
good-looking. Are they good-looking? 18 ③, ⑤
19 ① 20 I am. → we are 21 is a good boy.
22 is, is, are 23 ④, ⑤ 24 ⑤ 25 ①

02 주어가 복수이면 보어도 복수이다.

03 I와 함께 하면we로, you와 함께하면 you로 받는다.

04 bride는 여자이므로 she로 받는다.

05 ①, ②, ③은 지시형용사

08 ① he → him, ② my → me, ④ hers → her, ⑤ Their → They

11 her는 목적격과 소유격이 형태가 같다.

12 ④ Jane's → Jane

14 복수be동사는 are를 쓴다.

15 ② am → are

18 you로 물으면 I로 받는다.

19 those, these, they는 they로 받는다.

20 you는 너희들이므로, we로 받는다.

23 나라이름, 셀 수 없는 명사 앞에는 a를 붙일 수 없다.

25 ① is → are

01 ③, ⑤　02 ⑤　03 leaves　04 ④　05 ④

06 ①　07 cans, cartons　08 piece　09 ④

10 loaf → loaves　11 ①　12 ③　13 ④　14 ③

15 ④　16 ④　17 programmers → programmer

18 ③　19 ④　20 They are wonderful pets.

01 s, o, x, sh, ch로 끝나는 명사는 es를 붙여 복수형을 만든다.

02 '2개의 의자들'이므로 chair는 복수형으로 만든다.

03 f(e)로 끝나는 명사는 f를 v로 바꾸고 es를 붙여 복수형을 만든다.

04 classmates는 es를 붙여 복수형을 만든 것이 아니고 s를 붙여 복수형을 만든 것이므로 단수형은 classmate이다.

05 mouse의 복수형은 mice이다.

06 ②, ③, ④, ⑤는 셀 수 없는 명사이고 ①은 셀 수 있는 명사이다.

10 빵 4덩어리이므로 loaf의 복수형인 loaves가 되어야 한다.

11 모음(e)소리로 시작하는 단어 앞에는 an을 붙인다.

12 a(an)는 정해지지 않은 명사 앞에, the는 정해진 명사 앞에 오며, 고유명사 앞에는 관사(a,an,the)가 필요 없다.

13 세상에 하나밖에 없는 자연물에는 the를 붙인다.

14 ① 식사 이름 앞에는 the를 붙이지 않는다. ② 소유격 앞에는 a(an)을 붙이지 않는다. ③ 악기 앞에는 the를 붙인다. ④ 호텔 앞에는 the를 붙인다. ⑤ 운동 종목에는 the를 붙이지 않는다.

15 ⓑ 셀 수 없는 명사와 ④ 소유격 앞에는 a(an)를 붙이지 않는다.

16 단수동사 is가 나왔으므로 주어도 단수가 와야 한다.

17 주어가 단수이므로 보어도 단수가 되어야 한다.

18 she와 he의 복수형은 they이다.

19 복수동사 are가 나왔으므로 주어도 복수가 와야 한다.

20 It는 복수형인 they가 되어야 하고 is는 복수인 are가 되어야 하며, 보어 pet은 복수형인 pets가 되어야 한다.

01 ③　02 ⑤　03 ④　04 I　05 ⑤　06 ②

07 ②　08 ④　09 him → his　10 ③　11 ③

12 ⑤　13 ④　14 ②　15 ③　16 Is Seoul your hometown? → Seoul is not(isn't) your hometown.　17 ④　18 ③　19 ④　20 ③

01 ①, ②, ④, ⑤는 지시형용사이고 ③은 지시대명사이다.

02 지시형용사가 복수이면 뒤에 있는 명사도 복수가 되어야 한다.

04 We의 단수형은 I이다.

05 'the+단수명사'를 복수형으로 고치면 'the+복수명사'가 되어야 한다.

08 Jane은 나에게(me) 책을 준다. Tom은 항상 우리를(us) 찾는다.

10 ① Tom's:Tom의 (소유격) ② my father's:나의 아버지의 (소유격) ③ Maria's:Maria의 것(소유대명사) ④ Sumi's: Sumi의 (소유격) ⑤ Jane's:Jane의 (소유격)

11 ①, ②, ④, ⑤는 주어가 단수이므로 is를 쓰고, ③은 주어가 복수이므로 are를 써야 한다.

13 it+is→it's cf. its는 '그것의'라는 뜻으로, 소유격이다.

14 It는 3인칭 단수이므로 is를 써야 하고, Two bottles는 복수이므로 are를 써야 하며, Sugar는 셀 수 없는 명사이므로 is를 써야 한다.

15 ①, ②, ④, ⑤는 '~이다'이고 ③은 '~있다'이다.

17 'this'로 물으면 it으로 받아 주며, 내용상 '내 동생의 것'이라고 대답했으므로 부정의 대답인 No, it isn't가 알맞다.

18 your wife는 대명사 she로 받아야 하며, you(단수)로 물어보면 I로 대답한다.

19 대답의 주어가 they이므로 물음에서도 3인칭 복수주어가 나와야 한다.

20 보어가 dancers이므로 you는 복수주어이다. you(복수)로 물으면 we로 대답해야 한다.